Line managers have a key␣
individuals' potential, and this book forms a useful resource in their toolkit, helping them develop coaching skills, to navigate daily conversations. It demystifies the art of having a coaching conversation, making it simple to try out, and provides the reader with practical tools and support for everyday use.

   – Honey Clarke, director, HR,
      InfraRed Capital Partners Limited

Think like a Coach does what a lot of other books have tried and failed to do – make coaching something easily transferable to a manager's daily life. This outcome-focused model could revolutionise how we train people in the art of coaching and how we can truly embed coaching in our day-to-day management of teams. Gone are the days of learning abstract models in the classroom that have limited application outside a formal sit-down coaching session. For internal L&D leaders, this really solves the problem of 'What's in it for me?' that so often hinders our attempts to change manager behaviour.

   – Holly Jones, head of talent development,
      global construction company

Think Like a Coach is a beautifully simple guide to help new managers to develop and hone their coaching skills with lots of easy-to-apply practical steps. I love the Coaching Two-Step, where in listening and asking questions the coach can lead the team member to find their own answers.

– Clare Hill, CEO,
Sysdoc Limited

This book can act as your own pocket coach to help build your own coaching skills. Written in a simple, accessible way, it allows the reader to think and then act themselves into this vital role. Highlighting easy-to-apply techniques while encouraging people to develop their own authentic coaching style, this book will act as a reference for any new team manager and a refresher for others to grow coaching capability.

– Libby Gordon, CEO,
FARA Foundation

This book is very accessible and readable. The practical examples, case studies and avoidance of coaching speak make it quick for readers to apply the techniques. None of it feels like a giant step into something too different from what I do already. A few small changes, bringing some more consistency.

– Andy Morris, partner,
global professional services firm

Think Like a Coach is an absolute must-read for every new manager. It is without a doubt the best coaching book I've read and here's why:

1. It's easy to digest and dip in and out of as you need to. It was a real revelation to me to read such an accessible book.

2. It provides the reader with the confidence to try new approaches. It does this by breaking down areas of management that can feel overwhelming and scary for new managers, such as feedback, delegation and problem solving, and provides simple, practical, tried and tested techniques that will work every time.

3. Jude uses her own experiences and expertise to bring the examples to life and make them meaningful.

I'd loved to have read a book like this when I started my own management journey. For those of us a little nervous about how to manage teams to get the best results for everyone, this book shows you how to have the best, most productive conversations and assures you that you can do it!
    – Holly Williamson, head of people & purpose, global risk advisory, Deloitte

Managers need more resources like this – super practical, relevant and performance enhancing for both the manager and their team. Read this book when you first become a manager, and then read it again every time you get promoted. In fact, just keep it on your desk; if your week is filled with 1-2-1s, team meetings, catch-ups and feedback conversations, you'll use it every day. Jude has created a playbook for managing your team – it's more than a coaching manual for managers, and teaches you how to communicate with your team in a way that engages them and gets the best out of them.

– Rob Dighton, director,
 global professional services firm

I've been coaching and leading for 20 years, with advice and training aplenty along the way. But sometimes you need something you can navigate quickly for those in the moment coaching moments – and Jude's book is a perfect companion for those moments. Full of sharp wisdom and practical tips – a must for coaches and managers at all levels.

– Guy Johnson, head of quality and client policy,
 global law firm

To Ritu,
Stay Curious!

Jude

Empower your team through everyday conversations

THINK LIKE A COACH

JUDE SCLATER

Think Like a Coach
ISBN 978-1-915483-40-9 (paperback)
eISBN 978-1-915483-41-6

Published in 2024 by Right Book Press
Printed in the UK

© Jude Sclater 2024

The right of Jude Sclater to be identified as the author of this work has been asserted in accordance with the Copyright, Designs and Patents Act 1988.

A CIP record of this book is available from the British Library.

All rights reserved. No part of this book may be reproduced, stored in a retrieval system, or transmitted in any form or by any means, electronic, mechanical, photocopying, recording or otherwise, without the prior written permission of the copyright holder.

Contents

Introduction 1

Part 1: How to be coach-like

1 How to become a coach-like manager 11
2 The Coaching Two-Step 27
3 Coach-like questions 45

Part 2: The coach-like way to manage your team

4 Coaching in five minutes or less 53
5 Problem solving 59
6 Goal setting 69
7 Delegating 79
8 Catching up 87
9 Feedback 95
10 Strong emotions 105
11 Career conversations 113
12 Performance appraisals 121
13 Turning thinking into action 127
14 A way to practise with others 133
Conclusion 139

Question bank 143
Resources 154
Acknowledgements 159
About the author 160

Introduction

You already have the skills to conduct coach-like conversations. In essence, coaching is about listening, asking questions and talking to people.

As a busy new manager, I doubt you'll have time to find and read a 200+ page book or attend a day-long training programme. I waded through 75 pages of results on Amazon for 'books on coaching'. They all said they were for managers but when you dive into them, there's a lot of theory, models and acronyms – super interesting to read but not easy to remember or apply in real life. This book is different.

Coaching isn't as hard as you might think; you can't get it wrong and it doesn't need to be time consuming. I've created a model that busy new managers like you can start using immediately that will help you think like a coach. It uses skills you already have to be 'coach-like' in your everyday conversations.

What do I mean by coach-like? Here's a definition from coaching pioneer Sir John Whitmore: '[Coaching] is a way of leading and managing, a way of treating people, a way of thinking, a way of being.' (Whitmore 2017).

When a professional coach like me works with someone, it's done in private for a set amount of time. You can take the same coaching skills and use them in your everyday conversations with your team. This is what I mean by being coach-like. You don't need to be a professionally trained coach to benefit from using coaching skills as part of your management style.

For example, have you ever been stuck on a problem, gone to get help from a friend and then, while you're explaining the problem, realised you've worked it out for yourself? This is similar to how coaching works.

You find the answer yourself because, when your brain hears you talk out loud, it processes the information differently from when you think it through in your mind. You'd feel a bit silly talking out loud to yourself so your friend is a crucial part of your problem-solving process even though they might say nothing at all.

By giving you their complete attention, they've given you the exact help you need. Do you think you'd have found the answer if they'd interrupted you or kept on typing? Often all you need to get unstuck is to be able to think out loud with someone who cares and has the patience to let you come to your own solutions.

The top reasons to be a coach-like manager

It takes conscious effort to do something different, so there has to be something in it for you to make it worthwhile. Here are the top eight reasons I hear from managers who have adopted a coach-like style:

1. It **reduces your workload** by empowering your team to be self-sufficient so that they don't need to keep coming to you with every problem or decision.

2. You **identify problems early** because you're deliberately leaving space for your team members to tell you what's really going on.

3. Your team gives you **insight into how to manage them more effectively**.

4. It **takes the pressure off** you having to be the one with all the answers.

5. It's **developmental**, because coach-like conversations stretch people out of their comfort zones in a safe way, encouraging them to think and problem-solve for themselves by helping them learn from their own experiences.

6. It creates **instant commitment and responsibility** because the idea comes from them.

7. **Recruitment and retention are easier** because everyone wants to work with the manager who believes in their teams and helps them progress.

8. You get time for **your career development** because you have a high-performing team.

Ultimately, the reason managers adopt a coach-like approach is because it feels amazing. When you help someone come up with their own solutions it's empowering and energising for both of you.

Sami, a new line manager, found this with his team member Una, who was having a problem with a stakeholder. He called her into a meeting to find out what was going on so he could sort it out. Una thought the conversation with the stakeholder had been far worse than it was and, in the moment, Sami decided to try coach-like questions.

He learned that Una wasn't feeling as confident to challenge in this role as she had in her last one, which was news to him; he'd written her off as being unassertive. Together they explored what would need to change for her to feel more confident and what support she needed from him.

Sami was buzzing when he was telling me the story. He felt he 'got' Una so much more, their relationship had improved and Una had sorted out the problem herself. This wasn't the result of a planned, prepared-for coaching session. It was Sami listening to his instincts in the moment and giving coaching a go. It didn't need to be 'perfect'. It was coach-like and enough to change the outcome.

This book won't turn you into a coach but it will give you the structure and principles you need to think like one and give coaching a go as part of your everyday management style. I want you to take them, experiment with them and make them your own. You can't get it wrong. I know you can do it and I'm going to show you how.

Who this book is for

This book is for busy and overwhelmed new managers who are leading their first team. It will help you transition from being the technical expert to building a team of technical experts and it will help you develop a management style that will empower you to achieve your career goals.

Terminology

Throughout the book, I'll refer to you as the 'manager' and the person you're coaching as your 'team member'. This is for clarity and ease; in reality you can use these skills with almost anyone.

Where I've shared stories, these are either real in their entirety or a composite of real experiences, chosen to bring clarity to an idea. All the names have been changed.

How this book is organised

This book is your personal guide to being a coach-like manager and has been written so that you can find what you need as you need it. The contents page, end of chapter summaries and question bank make it easy to refresh your memory minutes before you meet with your team member – and the suggested experiments at the end of each chapter provide ideas about how to be coach-like every day.

Part 1 explains everything you need to know to have coach-like conversations with your team, including:

- a definition of what coaching is
- the mindset of a coach-like manager
- what psychological safety is, why it's important and how to create it
- how to coach using the Coaching Two-Step model
- how to ask coach-like questions that help your team come up with their own answers.

Part 2 is intended to be read just before you go into a conversation with your team member. It shows you how to use the Coaching Two-Step alongside other coaching knowledge and techniques to have coach-like conversations to:

Introduction

- **coach in five minutes** or less
- help your team members do the **problem solving**
- guide your team members to **set inspiring goals** they'll remember
- **delegate** using a coach-like style
- make **catch-ups** a developmental experience for you and your team members
- give **feedback**
- support a team member who's feeling **strong emotions**
- have **career conversations**
- make **performance appraisals** less 'tick box' and more developmental
- **turn thinking into action**.

It also includes a guide to how to practise with others so you can improve your skills while receiving personal coaching at the same time.

To help keep the ideas you're learning in this book alive you can also sign up for my weekly blog that goes out every Sunday morning (UK time) at thinkwithjude.com/signmeup. It has practical coaching ideas you can use every day.

> Boxes like this will pop up throughout the book to give you more details on a topic. For example, they might contain other points of view, extra tips or further explanation of terms. You won't miss any vital information if you skip these.

As you go through the book, my hope is that you'll give coaching a go and experiment with it. Because when you do, you'll notice just how capable your team can be and, most importantly, you'll get some time back to work on the things that light you up.

Part 1
How to be coach-like

1 How to become a coach-like manager

There isn't one clear, universal definition of coaching that everyone agrees on. So how on earth are you, a busy new manager, supposed to know what it means, let alone be able to put it into practice?

A *Harvard Business Review* study found that when managers were asked to coach someone with a time management issue, most struggled to stay silent and let the person work it out for themselves. Instead they gave advice or told them what to do (Milner & Milner 2018). It's no surprise that we default to telling: it's hard wired into us through our life experiences.

To paraphrase Whitmore (2017), when we were children, we did what the adults told us to do and lost privileges if we didn't. Then, at school, we did what our teachers told us to do and were put in detention if we didn't. Then we started work and did what our boss told us to do, or we could be fired if we didn't. So, when the time comes for us to be the boss, we do what comes naturally – we tell people what to do. It doesn't help that most of us think our job is to have all the answers and we don't feel we're adding value unless we do.

A definition of coaching for busy managers

I looked at many definitions of coaching and none seemed to explain in simple terms what it looks like when a manager is coaching. So I came up with the following:

Coaching is giving someone your attention while they think out loud and asking questions to help them discover their own solutions to act on.

This, in essence, is coaching and if this is all you remember, then like Sami in the introduction, you're well on your way to being able to coach as the moment arises. To expand on this a little more I'd like to introduce you to three related principles that underpin what it means to be coach-like:

1. Listen, don't fix

People want to feel heard so, when your team member comes to you with a problem – listen, don't fix. The value you bring is not your answers but a non-judgemental ear. Think about the times you've been interrupted with some well-meaning advice. How often was it helpful? How often do you do this to others? When you don't let your team member finish what they want to say, it sends a message to them that their thinking isn't as important as yours.

You can't think well if you feel inferior to someone so as much as possible let your team member finish speaking before you add your thoughts. If you need to interrupt, for example you have information that could be helpful, then ask for permission and wait to hear your team member say 'yes' before continuing (see Chapter 8).

2. Ask first, tell last
When you tell your team member what to do early on in a conversation you inadvertently make yourself the expert (Pedrick 2021). Without realising it, you're disempowering your team member and reducing their ability to come up with solutions on their own.

As amazing as I'm sure it is, your solution will never be as inspiring, creative and motivating as the ones your team member comes up with. As the manager, you'll always have space to add your thoughts later and when you do, offer them in a way that lets your team member know they get to choose if they want to take them on board or not.

3. Your team member leads the conversation
Your desire to help is often so strong that you jump in to solve your team member's problem before you fully understand what it is. That's disempowering for them and causes more work for you.

When you use a coach-like style you let your team member lead where the conversation goes so you can find out what's happening from their perspective. Letting them lead the conversation also means that the responsibility for the problem stays with them. This, in turn, builds their self-confidence and ability to make decisions without you.

The difference between coaching and mentoring

I have a confession to make. I hate the fact that 'coach' and 'coaching' have been used to describe the phenomenon of giving people space to think for themselves. What comes to mind for you as you read 'coach' or 'coaching'?

Managers tell me they think of a coach on the sports field: someone who has expertise in the sport and is telling the athlete what to do. And that's only one example. Unfortunately, the word 'coach' is now used in so many contexts that it's become murky, with lots of connotations.

To some people, coaching can feel a lot like therapy since they are both talking exercises. What makes them different is the recipient. In coaching the recipient is resourceful and whole; they are able to do what they need to reach their goals and aspirations. In therapy the recipient has lost their ability to be resourceful and the therapist is helping them make sense of their context, patterns and feelings to find new ways of being.

To provide clarity, I'm going to contrast coaching with mentoring.

Coaching	Mentoring
Asking	Telling
Unwavering attention	Sharing experiences
Listening to understand	Making suggestions
Using open questions	Offering guidance
Summarising	Giving advice
Sharing what you notice	Instructing

Mentoring is when you share your experience, advice, guidance and networks with someone else. You're doing the majority of the talking and that's helpful because your team member is learning from you by hearing about your approach, insights and mistakes.

Coaching is the opposite. Your team member is doing the majority – 70 per cent or more – of the talking. The benefits for you are huge. You'll gain insights into managing your team more effectively and identify problems early as well as find ways to develop your team to reduce your workload.

When to coach and when to mentor

First of all I want to make it clear that this doesn't mean coaching = good and mentoring = bad. In fact, as a manager I expect most of your conversations will involve a mix of both. Take a moment to consider where you might be on the scale in Figure 1.

Figure 1: Scale of coaching to mentoring

In the coaching skills workshops I deliver, most managers place themselves towards the mentoring side of the line. The purpose of this book is to show you how to shift towards the middle of that line so you have a greater range in your management style.

If you're curious to know when you might use a coaching style vs a mentoring style read the popout box opposite. It's a combination of ideas taken from Myles Downey (2015) and contributed by participants in coaching workshops I've delivered.

When to coach

- You don't know the answer.
- You want your team member to figure it out so they don't have to keep coming back to you.
- You believe your team member can figure it out themselves.
- You're curious and want to know more about what's going on.

When to mentor

- Your team member is tired or overwhelmed.
- When there's significant time pressure.
- Your team member is upset, stressed or panicking.*
- The task is complex and you're the expert.
- The task must be done in a specific way.**
- You have knowledge or personal experience that might help.

* In this state, your team member can't think clearly or creatively, so coaching is unhelpful. However, Chapter 10 explains a coach-like way to help them get back into a logical and rational state.

** Take a moment to consider if there's only one way to do the task or if you just want it done your way.

Some people will resist being coached. Marley, a director, came along to a coaching skills workshop to share their first experience of coaching. They explained that they used to get so annoyed when their manager would ask about their thoughts on how to approach a new situation. 'I just wanted to be told the answer because I was ambitious and wanted to progress quickly,' they said. 'Now I see that my manager was helping me to think for myself and I wouldn't have got far without that skill.'

Be persistent when coaching. Some people aren't used to being asked to think for themselves. And if you're ever unsure of which approach to take, then ask:

Do you want me to just listen, offer advice, coach you or something else?

How to switch from coaching to mentoring

The coach-like way to switch from coaching to mentoring so you can share knowledge and experience is to ask for permission:

I know something here that might help – can I share it with you?
I've had some experience of working with them – would it be useful if I told you about it?
This has happened to me too. Do you want to hear what I did?

Always wait for a reply and then share what you have to say. If they say no, and that rarely happens, let them know they can ask you about it later if they want to. Chapter 8 goes into more detail about the permission technique and how it works.

How to switch from mentoring to coaching

The coach-like way to switch from mentoring to coaching is to ask a question, for example:

What are your thoughts?
What do you think?
How might this help with your issue?

A fast way to work out whether you're on the mentoring side is to do a mental check of who's talking the most. Is it you? Yes? Then you're probably on the mentoring side. Mentoring is not wrong or bad. Remember, it's the style you're most familiar with and it will take some time for coaching to come naturally. As Rachel Hunter, a New Zealand model and ex-wife of Rod Stewart, said in a Pantene hair advertisement from the 1990s, 'It won't happen overnight but it will happen.'

Chapters 6 and 7 show more examples of how to move back and forth between coaching and mentoring.

The mindset of a coach-like manager

As the manager, what you expect of your team members will influence their performance. Expect more and you'll get more; expect less and that's what you'll get. These aren't absolutes, of course; if you expect too much you could be setting someone up to fail. I just want you to consider, if you have an underperforming team member, what role you might be playing in that.

Whether you mean it to or not, the way you think and feel about someone does influence the way you interact with them. As a character in Marilee Adams' leadership fable *Change Your Questions, Change Your Life* (2022) says, '[N]obody does their best work when their boss is expecting the worst from them.'

I learned the power of positive expectation when I was training subject matter experts to be in-house facilitators. Each participant had to deliver a training module to the rest of the class and they would get one-to-one feedback before trying again the next day. One participant, Siobhan, was clearly out of her depth and the session didn't go well. She knew it wasn't great and didn't need me to remind her.

In her feedback session I decided to focus only on what had gone well and we discussed how she could make more of her strengths. The next day Siobhan tried again, this time playing to her strengths – and the improvement was significant.

How to make it safe for coach-like conversations

As the manager, you have more power and authority than your team members. Even if you're part of the 'gang', there's always the possibility in their minds that you can use your power and authority if you want to. That can make it hard for your team to open up because they don't want to be seen as incompetent or, even worse, emotional in front of the boss. What you need to establish is psychological safety (Edmondson 2014).

Psychological safety is the belief that you won't be punished or humiliated for sharing ideas, questions, concerns or mistakes. You can't just tell someone, 'This is a safe space,' because only the individual can decide for themselves how safe they feel. What you can do is demonstrate this is a safe space through your words and actions.

I once worked in a consulting firm where the senior executives were also owners of the company (a bit like in a law or accounting firm). I walked into Peter's office and told him I thought his approach to an IT audit was wrong. He was a partner and I was a senior auditor, four grades below him, and he had a good 20 years more experience than I did. He could have used that to get rid of me.

Instead, he asked me to explain why I thought it was wrong and what I'd do instead. He didn't interrupt;

he listened and asked a few questions. By the end of the conversation, I realised he was right after all and, instead of feeling stupid, I felt I knew more than when I'd walked in. I also felt heard and respected and I bet Peter felt more confident in my abilities too.

Here are some suggestions from Amy Edmondson's research that you can use to show it's safe to have open conversations with you, even though you're the manager:

- Frame dilemmas that come up as opportunities for learning rather than blaming people for not delivering.

- Be vulnerable with the team and share your own failures and setbacks. Give them permission to tell you if they think you've missed something or made a mistake.

- Stay curious and ask questions to learn more.

Ultimately, to successfully adopt a coach-like style, you need to believe that your team member is capable of coming up with their own solutions. If you don't believe that, then stick to mentoring. However, if you want to challenge your assumption, you could try reflecting on this question: 'If I knew [team member] was capable of coming up with their own solutions, what might I do differently?'

Contracting to make difficult conversations easier

At the beginning of every new coaching relationship with a person, group or team, I make sure that we do some contracting. That's coach-speak for discussing ways of working. You might think, 'We're all adults, we don't need to do that.' But I once coached a team of senior leaders who said the same and then, three months later, they looked to me to tell one member they weren't pulling their weight.

Contracting is a way of establishing psychological safety by agreeing what's acceptable, what's not and how you'll manage problems when they arise. The 'ask first, tell last' principle is important in contracting because you move back and forth between coaching and mentoring using an 'ask, add, ask, add' pattern.

You can contract with your whole team as well as with each individual team member. Here's an example of how you might contract with a team member:

Ask: *How often do you want to catch up and for how long?*
Add: *Your thoughts.*

Ask: *How do you want us to structure our catch-ups?*
Add: *Your thoughts.*

Ask: *What would be useful for me to know about how you like to work?*
Add: *What would be useful for your team member to know about how you like to work?*

Ask: *What do you expect from me?*
Add: *What you expect of your team member.*

Ask: *What should we do if we feel like things aren't working between us?*
Add: *Your thoughts.*

It can seem awkward when you first have a contracting conversation, especially the question about what you'll both do if things aren't working – but after a while you'll feel awkward *not* doing it.

It's called contracting because it's a negotiation, so you don't have to accept everything your team member asks for. You could suggest trying something and coming back to reassess it in a few weeks' time. Contracting can be done at any time in a relationship and at a minimum I'd suggest discussing how it's working twice a year.

Suggested experiments

- Notice where you spend most of your time on the coaching to mentoring line. How might you spend more time in coaching?

- Choose one principle and try it this week in your conversations: 'listen, don't fix', 'ask first, tell last' or 'your team member leads the conversation'.

- Make a list of the ways in which you can demonstrate psychological safety and try one this week.

Summary

- A definition of coaching: coaching is giving someone your attention while they think out loud and asking questions to help them discover their own solutions to act on.

- The three coach-like principles are: 'listen, don't fix'; 'ask first, tell last'; 'your team member leads the conversation'.

- When you're coaching, your team member is doing the majority of the talking.

- Your conversations will involve a mix of coaching and mentoring. The coach-like way to switch to mentoring is to ask for permission; to switch to coaching, you ask a question.

- Your team members will live up to your expectations no matter how low they are.

- Create psychological safety by demonstrating your vulnerability and staying curious. Show your team it's safe enough to speak up without fear of punishment or humiliation.

- Consider contracting with your team members about how you'll work with each other, especially when things get hard.

2 The Coaching Two-Step

A boutique consulting firm I work with asked me to run a lunch 'n' learn session on coaching skills for their consultants. I wanted it to be practical but I only had an hour – not enough time to explain a coaching model and give people time to try it. Busy new managers need something they can recall and apply without needing to use huge amounts of brain power.

I was talking to a friend about it when I rather flippantly said, 'Coaching is simply listening and asking questions.' And in that moment, the basis for Coaching Two-Step was born. I say 'basis' because I was struggling to name the model. My husband commented that the way you step in and out was like a dance and he pushed for the Coaching Salsa. I wasn't convinced so he suggested the Coaching Two-Step instead. I liked it, my editor liked it and so here we are.

It's also a fabulous metaphor because coaching is like a dance. There's a structure to it and both parties move in partnership. I designed the model deliberately so that if you ever felt lost you could come back to the rhythm of it and no one would be any the wiser. As with any dance, you'll get more familiar with it as you practise; you'll add your own flair and make it your own.

I know that many organisations require their managers to develop coaching skills – and performance management systems are shifting emphasis from past performance to career management – but most training programmes are too ambitious. They try to teach a whole coaching model in half a day and expect managers to feel confident enough to try it on their team.

I completed more than 50 hours of coach training and practice and I was still nervous before I coached the first person who wasn't on my course. You don't need to be a trained coach to benefit from using coaching as part of your management style. I've stripped coaching back to the core skills you need to integrate it seamlessly into your everyday management style.

What is the Coaching Two-Step?

The Coaching Two-Step is a simple model that describes how you can be coach-like in any conversation, using skills you already have, such as:

- giving someone all your **attention** while you're listening to what they have to say
- keeping them talking by asking '**Tell me more**'
- **summarising** what you've heard to show you've been listening and understand.

Figure 2: The Coaching Two-Step

This takes the pressure off you to be the one with all the answers.

Grammatically speaking, it should read 'say/saying' tell me more but throughout the book I intentionally use 'ask/asking' because I want to convey a curious and interested tone. You're inviting your team member to keep talking aloud to give them space to find solutions themselves. You're replicating what happens when you solve a problem yourself when you're telling your friend about it. Also, as you'll see later, there are other ways of asking 'tell me more' that are questions.

In the definition of coaching, I specifically say it's about asking questions and yet questions aren't included in the model; I do that deliberately. The first questions you ask before you've understood the situation are usually either about the problem or are suggestions about what you think your team member should do.

They sound like 'Have you thought about getting up 20 minutes earlier?', 'Is there a way you could get your team to help with this?', 'Is it possible...?' or 'Do you think...?' I call these 'qu-gestions', ie suggestions cleverly disguised as questions. Although you don't mean them to be, they're full of judgement and likely to make your team member feel inadequate.

How to use the Coaching Two-Step

When your team member comes to you for help, stop what you're doing and give them all your attention, listening with curiosity to what they have to say. This is your starting position when coaching and honours the principle of 'listen, don't fix'. When they've finished talking, you have two options you can take:

1. Ask them to 'tell me more'.
2. Summarise the essence of what you've just heard.

These two options let your team member lead the conversation because they're free of judgement or opinion. Once you've tried one of these options, you go back to silently giving them all your attention while you listen with curiosity to what they have to say.

When they finish, you have the choice between the two options again and the conversation continues. If it were a dance it might look like this:

Figure 3: The Coaching Two-Step in action

Limiting yourself to these two options at the beginning of the coaching conversation helps you hold back your urge to be helpful. And by helpful, I mean solving the problem for them. Even if you were to offer a solution after only trying one option, at least you'd be closer to solving the right problem and you'd have a lot more insight into your team member and the team – like Sami in the introduction.

Try each option at least once, ideally twice, before you ask your first question. Chapter 3 explains how to ask questions to spark new thinking in your team member – helping them to think about their situation and what they have available to them in ways they hadn't considered before.

This is in line with the 'ask first, tell last' principle. Asking a question is like asking 'tell me more'; afterwards you go to attention, the starting position of the Coaching Two-Step, and use the two options to help your team member explore their thinking further. Try at least one option before asking a new question.

The best way to understand what being coach-like looks like is to see it in action, so I've included a demonstration you can refer to alongside this book at coachingtwostep.com/demo

Let's go through each part of the Coaching Two-Step so you can understand what each one is and how it works.

Attention

When was the last time you were able to talk without interruption or someone constantly checking their phone? I hope I'm wrong but I'm guessing it doesn't happen often.

Octavius Black and Sebastian Bailey tell a story in their book *Mind Gym: Relationships* (2009) about the time a friend went to a dinner party and was seated next to a woman they didn't like. He decided to play a game to see how long he could go by only showing positive body language and making positive 'mmm' sounds. After three hours the woman got up to leave and exclaimed, 'It was lovely sitting next to you. I'd forgotten how interesting you are.' The friend hadn't said a word.

The Coaching Two-Step

Attention is your starting position and the most important aspect because it helps your team member feel important and safe enough to think out loud with you without fear of punishment or humiliation (ie it contributes to psychological safety). Remember the example of going to your friend to solve a problem and they didn't say anything, they simply listened? You'll know you're coaching when you say very little and your team member says a lot.

When you're giving someone 100 per cent of your attention, it looks like this:

- listening to understand rather than to reply
- listening until someone has finished speaking before you speak
- being at ease and as if you have all the time in the world
- being present and focused on what your team member is saying so they can keep thinking.

The way people show their attention is different. For some it's being still, silent and holding eye contact. Others might look down because eye contact is disrespectful in their culture. Some people might need to take notes or fidget to be able to give their full attention. Do what works best for you and let your team member know that this is what attention looks like for you.

Dr Amishi Jha (2021) has a great analogy about attention being like a flashlight. You only have one flashlight and it can only ever be shining on one thing at a time. Whatever your flashlight is pointing to becomes brighter. So when you give your team member all your attention, they become brighter, because they feel safe enough to go where their thinking takes them.

People can tell when your attention is divided. It makes them feel unimportant, they doubt their thinking and they might give up or get angry – neither of which is going to help them find solutions.

If there's one thing I'd like you to do as a result of reading this book, it's to focus on improving the quality of your attention in those conversations that matter. If this is all you do, your relationships with your team members will improve dramatically.

Tell me more

The purpose of asking your team member 'tell me more' is to encourage them to keep thinking out loud. Remember that, if given space to talk out loud, your team member is more likely to solve their problem themselves. 'Tell me more' works well because it's curious, non-judgemental and doesn't lead the conversation with your assumptions or interpretations. The direction of the conversation is left to your team member, which is empowering for them.

Here are some alternatives to 'tell me more':

What else?
Say more.
What more do you want to say?
How do you feel about that?
What do you think about that?
What's most important for you?

Play around and experiment until you find what works best for you.

> ### 'Tell me more' – the debate
>
> The aim of this book is to make it easy to try coaching in your everyday conversations with your team members. As a professional coach I might phrase things in a way that may not sound natural if you said it, so I've been challenging myself to find alternatives that won't put you off.
>
> After reading former rocket scientist turned academic Ozan Varol's blog post, '3 counterintuitive ways to excel in conversation', I decided to use 'tell me more' because it comes from the world of interviewing, which most managers are familiar with, and it shows up on surveys all over the place so doesn't sound unusual. That said, some coaches disagree with using this phrase.

> Claire Pedrick (2021) argues against the 'me' in 'tell me more' because she believes it takes responsibility for finding the solution away from the person being coached. Clare Norman (2022) agrees, arguing, 'Tell me more might be processed unconsciously as, "Tell me everything I need to know to solve the problem for you."' She believes the purpose of a coaching conversation isn't to fill you in on what's happening; it's for the person to fill themselves in by accessing new thinking.
>
> Instead, Pedrick and Norman prefer to use 'Say more', or Norman suggests 'What meaning do you make of that?', which is an example of what I mean by wording that might not feel natural for you.
>
> My counterargument is that, as a manager, you do want your team member to fill you in on everything that's going on; it's your job to know so you can manage the team and its performance more effectively. A benefit of having coach-like conversations is that you find out a whole lot more than you do when you only give answers. I feel that Pedrick and Norman's concerns are more relevant for a professional coach than a manager who uses coach-like techniques to get the best from their team.

You don't need to worry that your team member will notice if you keep asking 'Tell me more'. I can assure you they won't. When someone is thinking for themselves, they don't notice the question – only the answers it sparks. If your team member does notice and says something, then the worst that will happen is that it'll be funny – and laughter is a great thinking energiser.

Summarise

When you summarise what you've heard, you show that you've been listening. Keep your summary short; you don't need to parrot everything back – just the essence of what you've heard. The more you're talking, the less your team member is thinking.

Hearing a summary of what they've said, especially hearing their own words, gives your team member another chance to hear their thoughts out loud and pick up any gaps in their thinking (Whitmore 2017). The managers I work with often realise how hard they are on themselves when I repeat back all they've achieved since the last time we met.

Another option, similar to asking 'Tell me more', is to ask your team member:

How would you summarise that?

This can be helpful if they've said a lot, because it forces them to pick out what's most important for them and means they continue to lead the conversation. It's also useful for you on that rare occasion when you accidentally shift your attention to what's for dinner that night.

Sometimes the most powerful summary is picking out a word and repeating it back with a question mark attached. For example, an assumption that keeps people stuck is their belief that they 'should' be doing something: 'I should be going to the gym every day', 'I should be able to do all these things', 'I should spend more time in the office'. When I hear statements like this I might say, 'Should?' They know what I mean.

Offer your support last

When you tell people how you'll help them, it takes away their power. It might make you feel good in the moment that you've reduced their discomfort but it makes the person you're 'helping' feel 'done to' rather than 'worked with' (Mannix 2021) They lose faith in their own abilities and a kind of learned helplessness, or feeling powerless to change things, kicks in where they can't do anything without first checking with you.

In Chapter 13, I go into more detail about the way to offer your support and want to remind you that the best help you can give is to help your team member figure out solutions for themselves. Remember – listen, don't fix. Offer your help at the end of the conversation when you're both clear on what support would be helpful. In this way your team member keeps hold of their power by asking for what they need and choosing what to take. Ask:

What support would you like from me?

Use more silence

As you've seen above, part of giving your attention is silence. When I run workshops on the Coaching Two-Step, the first exercise I get the participants to do is to listen to their partner talk for two minutes. They can't do anything else except listen. If their partner runs out of things to say, I ask them to hold the silence between them. They hate it. They say it feels cold, as if they aren't engaging with the other person – and they're right.

They're not engaging; they're leaving space for the other person to think. Remember to use your non-verbals, such as smiling supportively to show that you're listening while you're holding the silence. It's in the silence that the best thinking happens. Your team member needs those moments of silence to process what's going on before they can express their thoughts out loud. Silence also helps to slow a conversation down so that they can fully process everything that's coming up.

Silence can act like a question. I learned this one day as a new IT auditor. I had just gone back to Agnes from accounts for the third time with questions I'd missed the first two times. As I was looking down at my notebook, desperately trying to decipher what I'd written because I didn't want to come back for a fourth time, she blurted out, 'Joe has access, so he can check on things when I'm away.' Joe, the IT manager, should definitely not have had access to the finance system – a red flag from an auditor's perspective. If you want to know what's really going on, be silent.

An easy way to bring more silence into your conversations is to wait for two beats after your team member has finished speaking. It gives them space to follow their thoughts and gives you time to work out your next question without taking your attention away from them. And remember, you never need to worry about not having something to say because you can always fall back on asking 'Tell me more' or summarising.

Give the Coaching Two-Step a go

You now have everything you need to try a coach-like style with your team. Experiment with the skills in your everyday conversations and notice what happens. Like the participants on my workshops, it might feel unnatural and robotic at first, as if there's no engagement and flow as there is in a 'normal' conversation. And so it should – because this isn't a normal conversation. Your normal conversations – where you give your team all the answers and end up doing the work for them – are one of the reasons you're so busy.

Using a coach-like style is about having a different conversation so that both you and your team member benefit. The unnatural and robotic bit at the start is because I'm asking you to use your skills in a different way from what you're used to. You're learning a new dance and once you get used to it, it'll feel as natural and warm as your usual conversations, albeit still different.

I hope you'll give being coach-like a go. You can't get it wrong and the suggested experiments throughout this book give you easy ways to be a little more coach-like every day. So what if you try coaching and end up mentoring? That's OK. Notice it, think about what you could have done differently and move on. You're awesomely human.

Suggested experiments

- Give your team member your full attention, as if they're the only person in the room, until they finish speaking. What do you notice about the conversation?

- Ask 'Tell me more' in your next conversation and see what happens. Then try asking it twice and see what happens. Do you think the person noticed?

- Summarise the essence of what you heard back to your team member. What does your team member do when they've heard the summary?

Summary

- The Coaching Two-Step is made up of three skills you already have to help you conduct coach-like conversations with your team.

- Attention is the most important aspect because it creates the psychological safety your team member needs to be able to talk freely. It honours the principle of 'listen, don't fix'.

- 'Tell me more' and 'summarise' are ways of keeping your team member talking and thinking out loud in line with the principle of letting them lead the conversation. They also help with the principle of 'listen, don't fix'.

- Use each option at least once, ideally twice before you ask a question.
- Ask your team member to tell you what support they need from you, so they feel you're working together. See Chapter 13 for more.
- Silence is where all the thinking happens. It also acts as a question and slows the conversation down to give your team member space to process all their thoughts.
- Give coaching a go – you can't get it wrong. The suggested experiments are a good place to start.

3 Coach-like questions

Often the first questions you ask when someone comes to you with a problem are either ones that will help you solve the problem or 'qu-gestions' – suggestions about what to do disguised as questions. The benefit of being coach-like is that it takes the pressure off you to have the answers because by asking first and telling last, the answers are coming from your team member, which also increases their commitment and responsibility for action.

Coach-like questions spark your team member to think of things they hadn't considered before. They're often followed by silences when your team member's eyes will be looking up, down and all around to follow new thinking as it emerges. There might be stops and starts to speech as your team member is simultaneously talking and making sense of their thoughts. It's in this new thinking that your team member is going to find their answers.

All questions lead you into the attention position of the Coaching Two-Step. From there you have two options: asking your team member to 'tell me more' or summarising to encourage your team member to keep thinking. Use at least one option before asking another question to enable your team member to explore their thinking more.

Keep your questions short

Ideally your questions should be ten words or fewer. The more you're talking, the less your team member is thinking.

Ask outcome-focused questions

Coach-like questions tend to be outcome focused, meaning that you're asking your team member about what they want to happen in the future rather than asking them to talk about the past. Your team member already knows about their past and present but often they haven't thought about what their ideal solution would look like. You can't get to your destination if you don't know where it is, so start by asking questions such as:

What's your ideal outcome?
What do you want to happen here?
What's the best outcome for you?

Information is received in your brain through your senses. By asking your team member about what they might see, feel and hear, you're getting them to process all the data available to them to find new ways to approach the situation. Questions about your team member's senses might look like:

What would you be seeing happen if you got this outcome?
What would you be feeling if you got this outcome?
What would you be hearing if you got this outcome?

When your team member is crystal clear on what their ideal outcome is, they tend to find ways to get there a lot faster. Use the Coaching Two-Step to help them reach that level of clarity by using each of the options at least once if not twice before moving to the next question.

Choose questions that start with what

Questions that start with why tend to take you back to your childhood when your caregivers and teachers would ask 'Why did you do that?' when you were being told off. Consequently it tends to trigger a defensive response in many people so, even as a professional coach, I tend to default to questions that start with what. They're more likely to be taken as curious and free of judgement.

Here are some examples of how to reframe why questions into what questions.

Why question	Reframed as a what question
Why did you do that?	What was your thinking behind that action?
Why do you think they're not responding?	What do you think is causing them to be unresponsive?
Why is this annoying you?	What's important here for you?
Why don't you try...	What other options do you have? What else?

'Might' questions encourage curiosity

When you add 'might' to a question, it takes away the pressure of having to know the answer and instead invites curiosity and exploration. This also works brilliantly when two or more people are trying to solve a problem.

For example, what do you notice about your thinking when you hear 'What would be an ideal outcome here for us?' compared to 'What might be an ideal outcome here for us?'

Using 'might' seems to signal to people that they aren't bound by what they say and it's safe to voice all ideas that come up. It also invites playfulness and creativity and is a great way to get past blocks in thinking. Other great 'might' questions include:

How might we see this situation differently?
Who might be able to help us with this?
Where else might we be able to get what we need?

You can't get it wrong

Some questions will work better than others. This doesn't mean they're wrong, as long as your intention is to help your team member discover their own answers. Trust that the Coaching Two-Step will help your team member get to where they need to be. When I was learning to coach, I found it helpful to have questions to hand in case I went blank so all the questions I've suggested are grouped by chapter in the question bank at the end for easy reference.

Suggested experiments

- When a team member comes to you with a problem, ask them what their ideal outcome is before you say anything else.

- The next time you need to generate a lot of ideas in a meeting, try using a 'might' question.

Summary

- Questions lead you into the attention position of the Coaching Two-Step.
- The purpose of coach-like questions is to spark new thinking in your team member.
- Coach-like questions are short, about your team member's ideal outcome and mostly start with what.
- Get your team member to tap into their senses by asking questions about what they'll feel, see and hear when they achieve their ideal outcome.
- Adding 'might' to a question encourages creativity and generates more options.
- When your intention is to help your team member find their own solutions, you can't get it wrong.

Part 2
The coach-like way to manage your team

4 Coaching in five minutes or less

You're wired to think that telling someone what to do will be fast and that coaching takes too long. I'm here to bust that myth.

The Coaching Two-Step gives you a way to be coach-like in your everyday conversations, proving that it doesn't need to take hours and hours. If you're still worried, there's one more thing that will help. It's called a 'coaching container' and it focuses your team member's brain on what needs to happen in the time available – even if it's only five minutes.

Co-create a container for a coach-like conversation

Have you ever heard the old adage often called Parkinson's Law – 'Work expands to fill the time available'? Well, you could also say that coaching conversations expand to fill the time too because there's no defined time limit or container around them.

A coaching container sets out the boundaries of what's in and out of the coaching conversation. This is important because it focuses your team member's attention on the information that's going to help them solve their problem. A coaching container includes:

- the **topic** for the conversation
- the **time available** stated in the positive (see below)
- what **outcome** your team member wants from the conversation.

> **What does time stated in the positive mean?**
>
> People don't think clearly when they feel rushed, so being positive about the time you have, even if it's short, will bring a sense of ease into the conversation for both of you. 'I've got five minutes' feels a lot more spacious than 'I've only got five minutes'.
>
> When you clearly say how long you have, it makes it OK to check the time because your team member won't misinterpret it as disinterest (Mannix 2021). Being clear on time creates psychological safety because both you and your team member know you won't be late for the next part of your day (Norman 2022). As a result, you can be more at ease with each other in the time that you do have.

Here's an example of how to co-create a coaching container:

> **Team member:** *I'm dreading the conversation with Trudi about final payment.*
> **You:** *What are you dreading about it?*
> **Team member:** *They're going to try and bounce me back to their accounts payable but accounts payable already told me they're waiting on sign-off before they can process the invoice.*
> **You:** *Do you want to talk it through? I've got five minutes now.*
> **Team member:** *Yeah, that would be helpful.*
> **You:** *What's the question we need to answer?*
> **Team member:** *How do I get Trudi to approve the invoice?*
> **You:** *OK, so in the next five minutes you want to know how to get Trudi to approve the invoice for final payment?*
> **Team member:** *Yes.*
> **You:** *OK, where shall we start?*

In this example, your team member comes to you with a problem and you wrap that topic into the coaching container by stating how much time you have. The next step is to ask your team member about the outcome they want from the conversation so that they are leading it. You can do that by asking something like:

What do you want to get from this conversation? Where do you want to be by the end of this conversation?

Or, as you can see from that example above, you could ask what question your team member wants to answer. Nancy Kline, one of my favourite coaches, says the brain thinks best in the presence of a question (2011). That's because the brain is a connection machine and doesn't like to leave things unanswered – just like when a word that was on the tip of your tongue but you couldn't remember suddenly pops into your head later that day.

If your team member doesn't answer the question in the time you have, they will take it away and their brain will keep working on it. Finally, the manager repeats the container back to their team member to get agreement and then asks them where they want to start.

When I'm coaching, I notice that I can easily slip into 'tell mode' when I can see that time is almost up and the person doesn't have answers yet. Notice if this happens to you; it's OK if it does. You've been the one with all the answers for all of your career and it will take time for that urge to fade. Remember you don't have to have all the answers and your team member will be more committed to the answers they come up with themselves.

How to interrupt

Co-creating the container is extra important if your team member could talk all day without pause! As you're coming up to the end of the time, interrupt your team member and let them know how much time you still have (keeping it positive) and ask them what they want to do in that time. For example:

You: *I'm sorry to interrupt, I notice we have two minutes left. What would be most useful for us to do in this time?*

Norman (2022) also suggests regular time checks when you're having a longer conversation because when you refer back to the container it seems to inspire new thinking in your team member.

Suggested experiment

- If you're short on time, try having the conversation standing up.

This is a tip from my old project management days when I used to do 15-minute stand-up meetings every morning. One day I was sick of everyone complaining about it, so I let everyone sit down. The meeting went on for 40 minutes. The next day, everyone was happy to go back to standing.

Summary

- Co-creating a coaching container with your team member sets the boundaries for the conversation and focuses their attention on solutions.

- Tell your team member how much time you have, stated in the positive (eg 'we have five minutes'). This makes it OK to interrupt later.

- Ask your team member what they want to achieve in that time or what question they want to answer.

- Summarise what they want to achieve or the question they want to answer and restate the time available.

- Regular time checks inspire new thinking in your team member.

5 Problem solving

One way to reduce your workload and develop your team at the same time is to use a coach-like style to grow their capacity to problem-solve for themselves. In the moment, it feels like it will take forever but you know from Chapter 4 that it doesn't need to. And as Jayden, a manager in a workshop I ran commented, 'It feels great to see how much your team member has grown six months on, from figuring it out for themselves.'

When you solve your team member's problem for them, even if they ask you to, it means they might not be able to solve similar problems later on. When you let your team member lead the conversation so that they solve their problem themselves, they're more committed and take more responsibility for the outcome.

That means they don't have to come back to you as often. The Coaching Two-Step is a great way to help someone think through their problem and, if it's complicated or your team member is stuck, then using it alongside the coach-like questions below will guide your team member to new ideas.

Get to a clear ideal outcome

Being coach-like takes the pressure off you having to come up with the answers and that means you don't need to know anything about the problem or area of work to coach your team member. In fact, when you get your team member to give you all the context you're only having them go over the same thinking that has them stuck. If the answers were there they'd have them already.

Our natural tendency when someone comes to us with a problem is to ask questions about the problem. Here are two more reasons why that's not helpful:

1. Any solutions your team member comes up with are going to be influenced by the problem and probably won't be motivating.

2. Your brain will automatically try to find solutions, so your attention shifts away from your team member and onto solving the problem for them.

Let me show you with an example. Imagine your team member comes to you the day before a presentation they're due to give and they tell you they can't do it. You ask why and they tell you they're certain they'll screw up. So you ask questions such as 'What makes you think you're going to screw it up?' and 'What could you do so you don't screw it up?' These are great 'what' questions that use your team member's language and show you're listening. But because they're focused on the problem, they reinforce the idea of 'screwing up' and your team member will still only be thinking of ways to get out of the situation.

It's easy to get into fix-it mode when your questions are about the problem and before you know it, you're telling your team member what you think they should do. Instead, remember the principles of 'listen, don't fix' and 'ask first, tell last' to guide you on what to do. You'll often find that your team member has been so focused on their problem that they haven't even thought about what outcome they actually want.

By getting them to describe their ideal outcome, you highlight the gap between where they are now and where they want to be. This takes them into new thinking about how to bridge that gap. As a guide, you'll spend 60 to 70 per cent of your time here because when your team member is clear on their ideal outcome the steps to get there emerge quickly. Example questions you can adapt are:

In an ideal world, what would happen?
If we could wave a magic wand, what would be different tomorrow?
If it was an ideal day, what would it look like?
What do you want to achieve?
What do you really want?

Let each question lead you into the Coaching Two-Step and use the options to help your team member create a clear picture in their mind of their ideal outcome. Invite them to make it short and snappy – ten words or fewer – so that they're focusing on what's most important and can hold it in their mind. If they're unsure about their ideal outcome, get them to come back to you later. Their brain will keep working on it in the background.

In the scenario described above, an ideal outcome might be something like 'I come across as confident and knowledgeable'. You'll know when your team member has found their ideal outcome because it will look like a weight has been lifted from their shoulders and they'll speak with more enthusiasm and energy.

Uncover assumptions that are getting in the way

If your team member is still stuck after finding their ideal outcome, they might be assuming something that blocks their thinking. An assumption is something that you think is true but often isn't backed up by facts. To uncover any assumptions your team member might have, ask:

What might you be assuming that's getting in the way of [insert wording of ideal outcome]?

Problem solving

Follow this up with 'What else?' two to three times to help your team member list every assumption that's getting in their way and then ask:

Which assumption is most getting in your way?

This time, when you go into the Coaching Two-Step use 'tell me more' as a way for your team member to explore the assumption to see if it's true or not.

> **The difference between 'tell me more' and 'what else?'**
>
> As a general guide, I use 'tell me more' to go deeper into a topic and 'what else?' when I think going broader to generate lots of options would be more helpful. An easy way to remember which to use is to think of this T shape. Don't worry if you switch them round; it isn't wrong and your team member will eventually get where they need to.

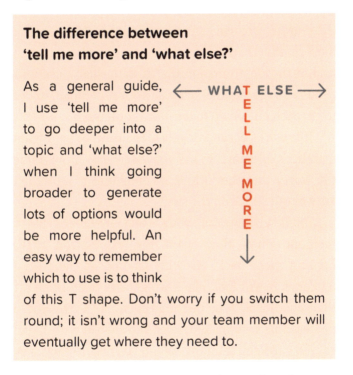

If your team member seems to be stuck and saying 'I don't know' a lot, then try this 'fill in the blank'

technique. It's one of my favourites because it's quick, easy to remember and works most of the time.

I'd really like to [fill in the blank] but [fill in the blank].

For example, 'I'd really like to come across as confident and knowledgeable but I'm worried I'll get questions I can't answer.'

We all tend to have a negativity bias, which means the reasons why we can't do something come to mind more easily than the reasons we can. Just as with finding the ideal outcome, the 'fill in the blank' sections need to be short and punchy, so ask your team member to get each one down to ten words or fewer.

This works because it gets to the heart of your team member's dilemma. In the above scenario, it might be the worry that they'll look incompetent if they can't answer questions on the spot.

You'll visibly see your team member's 'a-ha' moment when they voice the assumption that's holding them back. As with landing at their ideal outcome, it will look like a weight has been lifted off their shoulders. They might go silent for a moment to process this new insight; keep the silence with them, so they can keep thinking. When you're sure they have nothing more to say, use the Coaching Two-Step to explore the assumption further.

If your team member is still stuck

If your team member is still stuck, then these questions will jolt their thinking out of their problem and lead it towards solutions.

What advice would you give to a friend with a similar problem?

This one hardly ever fails to work. We humans love giving advice to others and it's usually the advice we need for ourselves.

What would you do if I wasn't here?

When your team members are used to relying on you, they don't stop to think how they'd solve things for themselves. This is a great question to use when you know they can handle the situation and are blocked because you've become their safety blanket.

What might you do if there were no limits?
If you knew you couldn't fail, what might you do?

When you ask your team member to imagine what their situation would be like if there were no constraints, their natural creativity kicks in and a world of possibilities opens up.

If your team member is still stuck, there might be

something they're not ready to admit to themselves just yet. Get them to sleep on it and come back to you. You've started their thinking and that will continue even when they walk away.

Suggested experiments

- When your team member comes to you with a problem, ask them questions about their ideal outcome before you try fixing it for them.

- Next time you get stuck, try the 'fill in the blank' technique on yourself and see if it helps — I'd really like to [fill in the blank] but [fill in the blank].

Summary

- Ask questions about your team member's ideal outcome. What do they ideally want to happen?

- When your team member seems stuck, ask them what they might be assuming that's getting in their way. When they've finished listing everything they can think of, ask them which assumption is most getting in their way and then use the Coaching Two-Step to explore the assumption.

- A simple technique to uncover assumptions is to ask your team member to fill in the blanks. I'd really like to [fill in the blank] but [fill in the blank].

- Jolt your team member's thinking out of their problem and towards solutions by asking questions about what advice they'd give to a friend, what they'd do if you weren't there and what they'd do if there were no limits.

- If they're still stuck, ask your team member to sleep on it.

6 Goal setting

When I think about goal setting in a work context, I cringe so hard I almost turn inside out. Below are real goals of mine from my corporate days and they all have the same things in common. They're vague, uninspiring and were never seen again until the following year:

- develop people management skills
- develop leadership and management ability
- run successful projects.

It's a shame, because a review of more than 35 years of research shows that goals do lead to better performance and job satisfaction (Locke & Latham 2002). Goals focus your attention and actions towards achieving what matters most to you and speed your growth by encouraging you to use your skills and knowledge in new ways.

The same review showed that the best goals are clear and specific (not vague like mine above), personal to you and reasonably difficult. Being coach-like will help your team set motivating goals they actually want to follow through on.

This is a conversation where you have a vested interest because their goals need to be in line with your goals as well as those of the organisation. Be open about that and if there's any misalignment, Chapter 5 might help you coach them through it. If your team member has an unrealistic goal, then Chapter 9 will be helpful. You'll be dancing back and forth between coaching and mentoring, so remember the principle of 'ask first, tell last'. Add your thoughts only after you understand your team member's perspective.

Make it meaningful

Your team member is only going to strive to reach a goal if there's something in it for them. It needs to fulfil their needs, desires and ambitions – otherwise, like my goals above, they'll sit in a closed document until it's once again performance appraisal time. Your team member's goals can still be meaningful, even if some of them have been set by you or the organisation, by connecting them to their career ambitions.

The first step is to help your team member uncover what's meaningful and important to them. This has the added benefit of giving them a reason to be committed to achieving their goals, even when things get tough. Try the questions below to lead you into the Coaching

Two-Step so you can use the options to get your team member to expand on their thinking:

What's the dream?
What would achieving this goal enable you to do?
What about the goal is so important for you?
What would it mean to you [to your family, friends, team, organisation] to achieve this?
What would be different if you achieved this?
What would you have that you don't have now?

You can help your team member to make their goal even more meaningful by asking sensory questions such as:

How will it feel to achieve your goal?
Imagine you've achieved your goal; what would you be seeing and hearing?

Had my manager taken me through this process with my goal of 'develop people management skills', then I might have realised sooner that I only said that because I wanted to be promoted. And I wanted to be promoted so that I could be involved in setting the learning strategy. Knowing that might have opened up other career possibilities.

Make sure the goal is framed in the positive so that their attention is focused on the result they want rather than the one they don't. A negatively framed goal might sound like 'None of my projects go over budget' as compared to the more positive and realistic 'My projects come in within ten per cent, plus or minus, of the budget'. If your team member's goal sounds negative you can ask:

If you were to frame that goal in the positive, what would that be?

Finally, make sure the goal is short so it's easy to remember by asking:

What would it sound like if your goal was ten words or fewer?

This process is similar to finding your team member's ideal outcome, which I covered in Chapter 5. The more time you spend here, the faster it will be to make the goal measurable and memorable. As a general guide, you might spend 15 to 20 minutes of a 30-minute session on this before moving on.

Make it measurable

Locke & Latham (2002) found that people are more likely to achieve their goals if they track their progress. To do this, you need to have some kind of measure. I love this question that I've adapted from Pedrick

(2021) as a way for your team member to work out theirs:

How will we know when you've achieved your goal?

This might sound weird but I get an answer every time. Or you could try what we coaches call a scale question. It works like this:

On a scale of 1 to 10, 1 being low and 10 being high, how close to [insert goal wording] are you right now?

For example: 'On a scale of 1 to 10, 1 being low and 10 being high, how close to setting the learning strategy are you now?' If your team member says anything over a 7, then you need to have a chat about whether this goal is inspiring enough. It might be, but it's worth checking. Next, follow up with:

Where do you want to be this time next year?

Your team member might say 10, or a lower number like 8. That's OK, it's their choice. Encourage your team member to aim for at least three points higher than where they are now so that there's enough challenge and stretch in the goal. This is important because goals need to be challenging to be successful (Locke & Latham 2002).

Scale measures are a handy way to check in with your team member in your catch-ups (see Chapter 8) because you can use them to track progress and talk about how to get from where they are now to the next point.

Make it memorable

While writing this book I had a picture of a book up on my wall with the working title and me as the author. Looking at it daily kept my goal front of mind. You're more likely to act on a goal that you can remember, so you have full permission to be playful and silly.

One manager I coached wanted to be known as a kind leader and was inspired by Jacinda Ardern, former prime minister of New Zealand. In difficult situations she would ask herself, 'What would Jacinda do?'

It doesn't matter if what your team member comes up with makes no sense to you; the aim is to help them find a way to keep their goal alive for them. Experiment with these questions and use the options in the Coaching Two-Step to help your team member explore ways in which to make their goal memorable.

> *What word or phrase best summarises the essence of your goal?*
> *What would make this memorable for you?*
> *What does your goal remind you of?*

If you know that your team member plays sport or loves music, you could try this question:

If your goal were a [insert their interest here] what would it be?

Ask what support your team member wants

To increase your team member's commitment to their goals, the best way to support them is to make them responsible for asking for the help they need rather than telling them what you think they need. Use these questions as a guide:

How can I best support you?
Where else can you get support?
How do you want to catch up about these goals?

You don't have to give them everything they ask for. It's OK to make other suggestions or take some time to consider alternatives and come back to them later.

Suggested experiments

- Try going through this process with your goals to see what you come up with. This would also be a good one to practise with others if you have formed a practice pair or trio as per Chapter 14.

- Try using a scale question in your next one-to-one. You could try:

  - How confident do you feel?

  - How complete is this project?

  - How supported do you feel?

Goal setting

Summary

- Goals work if they're clear, specific, meaningful and reasonably difficult.

- To build their commitment to their goal, spend a lot of time getting your team member to talk about it and why it's meaningful to them.

- Ask your team member to tell you how they'll know when they've achieved their goal. If it's intangible, use a scale question to get a sense of where they are now and where they want to get to.

- Help your team member come up with a memorable way to describe their goal so that it sticks in their head.

- To increase commitment and responsibility for the goal, ask your team member to tell you what support they need.

7 Delegating

The easiest way to reduce your workload and develop your team is to delegate. I say easy but fear of losing control or overloading your team, or thinking it's easier to do it yourself, often gets in the way. These obstacles are removed when you use a coach-like approach because you get:

- instant commitment and responsibility to the task
- an insight into their approach so you can catch problems early
- agreement on how to work with each other.

But you have to give up:

- mind reading and assuming your team's capacity
- your way being the only way
- micromanaging your team members
- fixing their work behind their backs.

When my coach challenged me to delegate more financial and marketing activities to my assistant it freed up a whole lot of time to write this book. I hadn't realised how much mental energy these seemingly quick tasks were taking up. I thought it was going to take at least a month to hand everything over but it only took a week! There'll be times when the tasks you're delegating aren't that interesting, so be honest about that. The chance for your team member to spend more time with you can often balance that out.

Co-create a delegating container

Just like with contracting in Chapter 1, you'll be moving between coaching and mentoring when creating a delegating container, using the same 'ask, add, ask, add' pattern. Another advantage of this pattern is that it lets your team member lead the conversation so they're more likely to take responsibility for what happens next. For example:

Ask: *How would you like me to brief you?*
Add: *Your thoughts*
Ask: *What else do you think you'll need?*
Add: *Your thoughts, if any.*

When you add, you're on the mentoring side. This is your chance to fill in any gaps, give advice or share your experiences. Then you ask your team member what questions they have or what they want to add, in line with the 'ask first, tell last' principle. In real life, it might look something like:

> **You:** *I'd like you to take the lead in recruiting a replacement for Dani. Would you be up for that?*
> **Team member:** *Yeah, it's something I've wanted to do for a while.*
> **You:** *Great, have you got 15 minutes now to go through it?*
> **Team member:** *Yes.*
> **You:** *How would you like me to brief you?*
> **Team member:** *I'm not sure.*
> **You:** *Can I make a suggestion?*
> **Team member:** *Yes.*
> **You:** *What if I give you an overview of the whole process now and then we talk through each stage in detail just before you get to it? How does that sound?*
> **Team member:** *Yeah, that sounds good. Is there documentation I can refer to as well?*
> **You:** *Yes, I'll send through the link after we've finished. What else do you think you'll need?*
> **Team member:** *Nothing at this stage but other things might come up as you're explaining the process to me.*
> **You:** *Great. Before we start, can we agree that you can stop me and ask me anything as we go*

through? I might slip into recruitment jargon without realising.
Team member: *Sure.*
You: *OK, so there are six stages in our recruitment process...*

Compared to a coaching conversation where you might talk 10-20 per cent of the time, in a delegating conversation it'll be more like 30-40 per cent of the time, because you need to add your knowledge of the task and any tips for success.

Before you go into a conversation to delegate, take a moment to think about what your team member needs to know and how prescriptive you need to be about the process. The more they can choose how to do the work, the more committed and responsible they'll be.

Check for understanding

The next logical step is to ask if your team member has any questions. The phrasing of this question is more important than you might think. In his blog post 'Yes, there are stupid questions', Ozan Varol explains that questions such as 'Do you have any questions?' or 'Do you know what I mean?' rarely get any response beyond yes or no – because who wants to look stupid in front of their manager? Instead, reframe the question and ask:

What questions do you have?

This signals to your team member that you expect them to ask questions and makes it safe for them to do so. Tell your team member this upfront so they're prepared for it, although remember that some people need to go away and come back with questions later. The questions your team member asks will give you an opportunity to spot any problems early and give you an insight into how to manage them more effectively.

When your team member asks you a question, your natural impulse will be to answer it and – quick as a flash – you'll get stuck in telling them what to do. Pause before answering to consider if this is a question that you need to answer or if this is a coaching opportunity. You don't need to turn every question into a coaching opportunity, though – it'll drive your team members mad. Here are some other questions you can use to check their understanding:

What are your thoughts on how you'll approach this?
What concerns do you have?
What challenges do you see already?
What else do you need to know from me?
What else are you working on and how might that impact this project/task?

Use each option of the Coaching Two-Step to get your team member to expand on their answers so you can be extra confident they're on the right track.

Delegating is also a good opportunity for development:

> *Which of your strengths are you going to draw on for this?*
> *What do you want to learn from this?*
> *What skills or knowledge do you think you need to do this that you don't have yet?*

Following the principle of 'ask first, tell last', be sure to add your thoughts as well. This is a good time to encourage your team member and demonstrate how much you believe in them.

Contract for how to work with each other

As you saw in Chapter 1, contracting helps you and your team member agree how you'll work together. It works because it's a vulnerable conversation where you both have to admit things might get rough and you both have to agree what you'll do in that situation. It creates the psychological safety needed to speak up when things get crunchy and reduces uncertainty by giving you a process to follow. See Chapter 1 for a guide.

Suggested experiments

- In your next one-to-one with your team, ask them what capacity they have to take on more and what they'd like to be doing.

- Next time you explain something to someone, try asking 'What questions do you have?' instead of 'Do you have any questions?'

Summary

- When your team member leads the conversation, it creates instant commitment and responsibility for what will happen next.

- Co-create a delegating container by using the 'ask, add, ask, add' pattern:

    - **ask** your team member how they'd like to have the conversation

    - **add** your thoughts

    - **ask** your team member what more they'd like to add

    - **add** your thoughts, if any.

- You'll be talking 30–40 per cent of the time.

- Ask your team member what questions they have.

- Use questions to check their understanding, knowledge and approach so you can catch problems early and get insight into how to effectively manage your team member.

- Agree with each other when, where and how often you'll catch up, what needs to be escalated to you immediately and what they can handle on their own.

8 Catching up

When you approach them in a coach-like way, catch-ups become developmental. By asking your team members to self-evaluate their progress, they end up becoming much more self-reliant. That means they take on more responsibility and take up less of your time.

Like coaching, catch-ups don't need to be formal, scheduled events – they can happen at any time, in any place. One of my early managers used to ask me catch-up questions when we were going to or from a client meeting; he was literally making sure I was learning on the job. Of course, I think this was also a time-saving measure for him but it worked for me and I'm forever grateful for his attention to my career growth.

Self-evaluation questions

I suggest starting your catch-ups with self-evaluation questions, otherwise they get taken over by updating on progress and the opportunity for learning is lost. In a 30-minute catch-up you might spend 10 minutes asking questions like these that help your team member become aware of their strengths, competence and problem-solving ability:

> *The last time we spoke about this you said you were a 4 on a scale of 1 to 10. Where are you now? Then: What did you do that got you there? Then: What would make it a [one number higher]?*
> *What are you most happy about?*
> *What's working well and why?*
> *What are you learning about yourself?*
> *What challenges have you overcome and how?*
> *What strengths are you noticing? Where else could you be using these?*
> *If you could do it again, what would you do differently?*
> *How are you going to celebrate your success?*

Asking about challenges also creates an opportunity to coach your team member through them. Remember, you don't need to have all the answers – you're helping them figure it out for themselves.

> *What's been the hardest bit?*
> *What challenges are you facing?*
> *What are you stuck on?*

All these questions lead into the Coaching Two-Step, where the options give you a way to help your team member come up with solutions. This is also a good time to encourage your team members to take a moment to acknowledge their part in what has gone well.

Remember that humans tend to have a negativity bias; we remember the bad more easily than the good. Giving your team member a chance to recognise what's gone well helps to build their self-confidence and self-esteem. It works for busy new managers too.

How to get feedback

One-to-ones with your team members are also a good opportunity for you to get feedback for your own career development. These questions give you that as well as being an empowering way to delegate responsibility to your team members to work out on their own when they need you and when they don't:

> *Where would you like me to be more or less involved?*
> *What do you see me getting involved in that I don't need to?*

These sorts of questions work for three reasons:

1. You're asking for **feedback on something specific**. One of the reasons you might not receive good quality feedback from your team is because

you ask closed, broad questions such as 'Do you have any feedback for me?' This kind of question almost always gets a 'no' response. When asked out of the blue, it also puts your team member on the spot.

2. You sound as if you're **asking for advice** – and everyone loves giving advice.

3. You make it **safe** to give feedback. The questions are framed positively so your team members can tell you what frustrates them about your management style without having to directly challenge you.

Listening to the feedback doesn't mean you have to take it – like your team member, you have a choice. And you're creating psychological safety in your team because it's a lot easier to take difficult feedback from your manager when they ask for it from you.

Ask for permission to share your thoughts

You'll move back and forth between coaching and mentoring in a catch-up conversation because, as well as getting your team member to self-evaluate, you need to offer your feedback as well. A way to do this so that your team member is leading the conversation is to ask for permission. For example:

Catching up

Can I make a suggestion?
Can I share something I'm noticing?
I know something that might help here. Can I share it?
Would it be helpful if I told you how I've done this in the past?
Can I tell you about what's not working for me?
Can I share what I'd like to see you doing more of?

Asking for permission works because it:

- **focuses** your team member's **attention** on what you're about to say
- **gives** your team member a **choice** and leaves them in control of the conversation
- **shows your vulnerability** – your team member could say no, so this contributes to psychological safety
- **mitigates the power imbalance** between you because your team member is leading the conversation
- tells your team member they're an **equal partner** in the conversation.

It'll only work if you wait to hear your team member's response – otherwise you're giving them a choice when there isn't one. If your team member says no, and I've only had this happen a handful of times in more than a decade, then let it go. Tell them they can come back to you when they're ready.

When you've finished sharing your thoughts, ask your team member a question to shift back to the coaching side. For example:

How might that be useful for you?
What has changed for you now you've heard that?
What ideas have come to mind now?

Completing the catch-up

Leave five minutes at the end of your catch-up to ask your team member:

What else do you want to talk about?

This gives them one more chance to raise anything else that might be bubbling under the surface and you a chance to catch a problem early. It might be that they have something on their mind and aren't sure if they should raise it with you, or they haven't thought it through yet. So give them that chance. They might be feeling more confident now that they know the purpose of the meeting is to catch up and not catch them out.

Suggested experiments

- Tell your team member what you're going to ask before your catch-up so that they can think about their answers. It also makes it normal for you to have the questions in front of you.

- In your next catch-up with your team member, ask them at the end what else they want to talk about and notice what happens.

Summary

- Start by getting your team member to tell you what's been going on, what they're proud of and what's challenging them. This will help them become more aware of their strengths, competence and problem-solving ability.

- Ask for feedback on where your team member would like more or less involvement from you. This helps them take more responsibility for asking for help and gives you information to help with your career development.

- Ask for permission to share your thoughts. When you've given your thoughts, ask a question to move back to coaching.

- Before the end of your catch-up, ask your team member what else they want to talk about in case there's something they haven't brought up yet.

9 Feedback

One of the biggest fears about giving difficult feedback is how the other person will react. In this chapter I'll explain what triggers negative reactions and show you a coach-like way to give feedback that reduces their intensity.

The greater the psychological safety between you and your team member, the easier it will be, so I highly recommend trying out contracting from Chapter 1 and the 'feedback for you' questions in Chapter 8. It's a lot easier to take difficult feedback from your manager when they ask for it from you.

The fight, flight, freeze response

When faced with a threat, you have three automatic survival responses:

1. **fight** – step in and face the situation head on
2. **flight** – get out of the situation as quickly as possible
3. **freeze** – be as still as possible and hope the threat passes you by.

When your body goes into survival mode, rational and critical thinking are sidelined so all of its resources are ready for one of these responses (the FFF response for short – Peters 2013).

Even if you don't mean it to be, difficult feedback may be perceived by your team member as an attack, so it might trigger their FFF response. If this happens, let your team member lead the conversation by asking them how they want to continue. They might need some time to absorb the message before they can discuss it with you.

I know that when I'm pulled up on something that's way out of line with my values, my embarrassment comes out as defensiveness, so I need some time to cool off before I can talk about it rationally. This might be something you contract with your team member about. Also see Chapter 10.

> **The impact of mystery meetings**
>
> I don't know how many times I've walked into a meeting worried about being told off, only to find I was being given a new project to work on. When the brain doesn't have the full information, it makes up the worst-case scenario, which triggers a FFF response. Don't put mystery meetings in your team member's calendar to have a 'chat'. Give them some context.

What if you feel your FFF response is threatening to hijack you? Here's a little trick from Christopher Bergland (2019) to hack your vagus nerve, which is responsible for getting your body ready to respond to threats. Slow your breathing so that your exhale is longer than your inhale. What this does is tell your mind that everything is OK, so the vagus nerve takes your body off high alert and slows your heart rate, bringing you back to a calm state. The cool thing is that you can breathe in this way and no one will notice.

Framing feedback and asking for permission

To reduce the intensity of difficult feedback, frame the conversation in a way that gives your team member context and a choice over whether to hear it. In this way you're using the principles of your team member leading the conversation and 'ask first, tell last' to approach the conversation in a coach-like way. For example:

> *I want to tell you about something that's affecting your chances of promotion because if it were me I'd want to know so I could do something about it. Before I do, I want you to know that I'm here to support you in any way I can. Do you want to hear it?*

This frame has four elements:

1. **Context:** *I want to tell you about something that's affecting your chances of promotion.*

The frame works because it immediately tells your team member what's in it for them to have this conversation. It also creates certainty for your team member – they know what they're getting into and it reduces the likelihood of their FFF response kicking in before you've even started.

Think of it like this: how would you feel if you were given a tin can with no label and told you had to eat whatever was inside? Uncertainty sparks the FFF response, which results in an inability to think because all your body's resources have shifted to survival mode. Always give context.

If you have contracted with your team member (refer to Chapter 1), then your frame might start with something like 'I know it's important to you to get promoted and we agreed I'd tell you immediately if anything was getting in the way so we could work together to address it. Is now a good time?'

2. **Empathy:** *because if it were me I'd want to know so I could do something about it.*

This is you being human. No one likes giving bad news, so by acknowledging that the message isn't going to be easy, you show you respect and believe in your team member enough to have the conversation regardless of the difficulty. If you didn't think they could change, you wouldn't bother. This also shows that you understand how vulnerable someone can feel in these kinds of conversations, thereby reinforcing psychological safety.

3. **Support:** *Before I do, I want you to know that I'm here to support you in any way I can.*

On its own, feedback is only information and it's not always clear to your team member what actions to take as a result. I know an organisation that has an amazing 360-degree feedback process that everyone goes through twice a year. The problem is there's no support to address the feedback, so the same issues come up in each review.

Awareness doesn't automatically equal action and change, especially when there's no support to work out what the action is. If you're not up for helping your team member, then question whether you should be giving the feedback at all. Is it more about you than them?

4. **Permission:** *Do you want to hear it?*

Asking for permission before you share the feedback lets your team member lead the conversation and demonstrates psychological safety by giving your team member a choice. They become part of the conversation rather than the target of it. So it's vital that, after asking, you pause and wait to hear their answer.

When they say 'yes', you'll know you have their attention and can give the feedback. If they say 'no' - and this hardly ever happens - you can ask them why: 'I understand you don't want the feedback now. Can I ask why?' It could be that the time and place aren't right and you can agree to meet up later or move somewhere else. Make sure you're giving your team member plenty of room to make their own decisions so they'll be receptive to the feedback - otherwise it won't stick.

Asking for permission sounds weird but it works. See Chapter 8 for more detail on how and why.

Example frames

Here are some other example frames that you might find useful:

- When you need to talk about actions that go against the team or individual contract:
  I'm noticing lately that you're doing things that aren't in line with our contract and I'm curious about what's going on and how I might support you. Is now a good time to talk?

- When your team member is overconfident and making mistakes:

I want to talk to you about your recent work. I'm noticing a pattern of errors so I'd like to talk them through with you and find out how I can better support you. Do you want to talk about it now or later?

If your team member says later, make sure to put a specific date in the diary and keep to it. You are responsible for managing poor performance and, while you can do that in a coach-like way, your management responsibility comes first.

- When someone refuses to come into the office, even for specific events:
I saw that you declined the invite for the onsite meeting and I'd like to talk to you about that. I want you there because the newer members of the team are missing out by not being able to learn from you and I'd like to see if we can come to an agreement about when you come into the office. When would be a good time to talk this through?

Make your feedback short, direct and clear

No matter how hard you try or how many words you use, you can't predict how someone will react to difficult feedback. One day they might take it well and another they might get defensive; it all depends on what's going on for them. All you can do is give the message as clearly as possible. As Brené Brown says (2018), 'Clear is kind, unclear is unkind.'

Here's a classic example of an unclear message:

> So, you know when you present to the stakeholders, well, and I know you don't mean to do this or anything, it's just that, well, and you're totally doing a great job of leading this project. It's just that when you're asked questions you get a bit defensive and it reduces their confidence in you. It's not just you, though, and like I said you're doing a great job.

There's no doubt the manager has good intentions; they want to be nice and not hurt their team member's feelings. But all this kind of feedback does is leave your team member confused, dismissive, defensive, in tears or obsessing over it. Clear and kind sounds more like:

> In the last two stakeholder meetings, I notice the answers you give to their questions come across as defensive and they're starting to perceive you as a difficult person to work with. I'm curious: what's going on for you in those meetings?
>
> Here the manager clearly states the facts without judgement and the team member is being asked for their side of the story. Remember to listen, don't fix as you're giving them all your attention and use the Coaching Two-Step to explore what's going on.

Suggested experiments

- Next time you feel your own FFF response being triggered, practise breathing so your exhale is longer than your inhale. For example, breathe in for four counts and out for six counts. Do this three times. How do you feel?

- Prepare a frame for your next feedback conversation.

Summary

- When the brain perceives a threat, such as feedback, it triggers the fight, flight, freeze (FFF) response. The emotional centre of the brain takes over and your team member won't be able to respond in a rational way.

- If your team member has a strong reaction to the feedback, ask them how they want to continue; let them lead the conversation.

- You can calm your own FFF response by breathing out for longer than you breathe in.

- When giving feedback, frame it using the four elements:

  1. context – say what the conversation is about

  2. empathy – show that you know it'll be hard to hear

  3. support – explain that you're here to help

  4. permission – ask if your team member wants to hear it and wait for their answer before giving the feedback. If your team member says 'no', ask why and assure them they can come back to you.

10 Strong emotions

Let's make it OK to express feelings at work – all of them. All that happens when you ask people to leave their feelings at the door is that they burst out in unexpected ways. When you allow your team to express their feelings at work, you create a psychologically safe environment in which they're more engaged, creative and innovative (David 2018). That means your team tell you about problems early and will go the extra mile for you because you care.

Strong emotions trigger the FFF response and in this state your team member can't think clearly (refer to Chapter 9 for more). Instead, their limbic system – the part of the brain that processes information with feelings and acts on instinct – takes over (Peters 2013).

One time, when I was fresh out of coaching training, Daisy, a good friend and colleague received news that something had gone wrong on her project. As tears filled her eyes, I took her out to the stairwell for some privacy and tried some of my best coaching questions. She looked me dead in the eye and said,

'I don't need a coach right now, I need a friend.' So I comforted her and listened. Then she asked me to tell her what I thought she should do next, and I did.

You can't coach someone in a high emotional state but you can use the coach-like principles – your team member leads the conversation, 'ask first, tell last' and 'listen, don't fix' – to help calm their limbic brain so they can think clearly again.

Ask your team member what's on their mind

It's even more important to let your team member lead the conversation when they're in their FFF response, otherwise the lack of control will push them further into it. Ask a big open question, such as:

What's on your mind?
What's up?
What's really going on?

Michael Bungay Stanier (2016) explains that these work because:

- they're open and invite your team member to share what they think is most important
- they allow your team member to choose what to share so they can lead the conversation

- they work like a release valve for whatever is taking your team member's attention and energy.

One year I was in New Zealand for a close friend's wedding. She came to pick me up from where I was staying and, before she'd even crossed the road, I could see she was crying. The wedding was in one week and she was overwhelmed by how much she had to do. Once we got back to hers, I asked her to tell me everything on her mind and each time she stopped talking, I asked, 'OK, what else?'

As she spoke, I wrote down what she was saying and, when she didn't have any more to say, I showed her the list. She looked at it, smiled and said, 'Oh, there's really not much to do, is there?' When your team member can see all their thoughts on paper, they don't have to use energy to hold everything in their head. Like my friend, once they can release the emotion they're feeling, they relax and their brain is free to be rational, logical and creative again.

Acknowledge that what your team member feels is real

This isn't the time to talk about your own struggles or to 'silver line' your team member's experience. That's when you tell people to look on the bright side, and it sounds like 'At least...' or 'If it makes you feel better...' Remember – listen, don't fix.

Also avoid telling your team member that everything will be OK or making comments such as 'You've got this'. It risks making your team member feel unsupported and as though they aren't good enough to handle the pressures of their job. Instead, acknowledge how hard it must be for your team member and give them lots of space to talk about what's going on, with a response such as:

That sounds really hard; thanks for telling me.

If you feel comfortable exploring your team member's feelings, then you could ask:

What are these feelings telling you?

Our emotions usually hold some message for us based on our experiences. By asking your team member to take a moment to tune into their feelings, you're also gently encouraging them to tap into their intuition and trust their instincts (Fosslien & West Duffy 2019).

For example, anger might indicate something is important to them, or impatience might suggest a self-imposed deadline that no one else knows about. Some people might not have the emotional awareness to answer this question, so if they say they don't know, tell them that's OK – and move on to asking what they need.

What to do if your team member cries

No one wants to cry at work, so let your team member know this is completely normal by sitting with them while they cry, offering a tissue (if you have one) and being silent. Hold back your impulse to rescue them and don't make statements intended to soothe their distress, such as 'I'm sure it'll all be OK' or 'At least [anything]'. All this does is diminish your team member and tell them that this *isn't* a safe space to express their emotions (Mannix 2021).

You can't make it better and your team member isn't expecting you to either. The best you can do is to be with them so they can express what they're feeling. When you do this, you make your team member's outpouring of vulnerability OK and that strengthens the psychological safety between you.

I know it can be uncomfortable to sit with someone while they're crying – but it's not great for them either. Reassure your team member when they apologise for crying that it's OK and there's no need to apologise; this is normal. Crying doesn't always equal sadness; in the workplace it could be a signal you care about your work or a sign of anger and frustration (Fosslien & West Duffy 2019). Some people rant; some people cry.

Let your team member ask for help

Trying to fix your team member's problem or deciding what should happen next sends a message that you don't think your team member can handle the situation on their own. This keeps them in their FFF response and damages the psychological safety you have between you. Trust that your team member knows what they need and let them tell you, rather than making knee-jerk reactions and offering things they don't need.

What help would be most useful from me right now?

Your team member doesn't need to be saved. They need to be heard and, if you have a suggestion, ask for permission to share it so that they continue to lead the conversation. Also, check where else your team member is getting support so that it's not all landing on your shoulders.

Where else are you getting support?
Who else can you get support from?

Suggested experiment

👤 Take your conversation outside for a walk.

People are more comfortable talking about challenging things when walking side by side because they feel less judgement and pressure to talk when they're not being stared at (Burn 2020). Additionally, research summarised by Kirsten Weir (2021) for the American Psychological Association suggests being outdoors reduces feelings of stress and boosts mood. If you can't be together, then do what Clare Norman suggested to me – talk to your team member on the phone while you're both out for a walk.

Summary

- Start with an open question such as 'What's on your mind?' to encourage your team member to tell you what's going on for them.

- Acknowledge what your team member is feeling and thank them for telling you.

- Crying is a normal and natural way to express emotion. When your team member cries, reassure them it's OK and trust them to tell you what they want to do next.

- Ask your team member what support they would like and where else they're getting help.

11 Career conversations

A career conversation is exactly what it sounds like: a conversation with your team member about their career. Despite taking extra time out of your day, the benefits in terms of motivation and retention are huge. Those who have fewer career conversations are less satisfied in their role and 31 per cent of workers quit because there aren't opportunities for progression, upskilling or reskilling (LHH 2022).

It's no wonder many organisations are ditching performance appraisals in favour of career conversations to recruit and retain staff. They're a way of showing your team members you care about them, not just about getting the job done.

These are also a great opportunity to experiment with being coach-like because the purpose is to give your team member some time out from their work to think about how they want their career to develop. You don't have to be the one with the answers – they do.

Ask your team member if they want to have a career conversation

This may seem a little odd but you're not responsible for your team member's career – they are. One way to build that responsibility in them is to give them the choice whether or not to have a career conversation.

Set aside specific times for career conversations

When career conversations are added to regular catch-ups, they either don't happen or are rushed. Agree a specific time with each team member in addition to regular catch-ups to talk about their career. Try for once a quarter or at least twice a year as a minimum and agree that no work stuff is allowed.

Talk about the past, then the future, then the present

We don't usually delve much into the past when coaching but career conversations are an exception. Usually, people haven't thought a lot about their career and the twists and turns that brought them to where they are now. By asking your team member to describe their career it helps you both to understand their motivations and values as well as being a rich source of experiences to learn from when they're thinking about their next career step. Try asking questions like these to further explore your team member's career:

What are you most proud of in your career?
If you could go back, what would you change?
What has your career to date taught you?
How did you make the decision to move roles or organisations?
What did changing roles or organisations tell you about what you like or dislike about work?

Each question takes you into the Coaching Two-Step, where you can use the options to help develop your team member's awareness. This might be the first time they've ever talked about their career out loud, so they could be discovering things about themselves for the first time. Using the principle of 'ask first, tell last', hold back your thoughts until you've heard your team member so that you gain plenty of great insight into how to manage them.

Once you've covered the past, it's time to talk about the future, just like you do in other conversations when you're asking your team member for their ideal outcome (see Chapters 3 and 5). Let your team member lead the conversation by asking them to pick a time frame that works for them.

Some people are comfortable talking about the next five years; others don't think beyond the next month. In that case, gently encourage your team member to think at least a year ahead. And unless your team member brings it up, don't ask what their career aspirations are, as that seems to trigger a freeze response in a lot of people. Instead, try questions (and prompts) such as:

> *Describe your dream career.*
> *What would you like your career to look like in the future?*
> *What do you want more of in your career?*
> *What do you want less of in your career?*

Get your team member to write down these answers somewhere they can refer back to when making career decisions. I found an old notebook from 2012 where I described the elements of my dream career and I'm now living it.

Finally, ask your team member what's happening in their career now to help them plan their next steps:

> *What's going well in your career?*
> *Where would you like to focus your attention?*
> *What skills do you want to develop?*
> *What opportunities do you need?*
> *Who do you need to build stronger relationships with?*

The principle of 'listen, don't fix' is important here because you don't want to end up with responsibility for your team member's career. Chapter 13 explains how to offer your support.

Check in about how the conversation went

You might feel awkward about asking for feedback about your coaching, which is why I've included Chapter 14: A way to practise with others. However, this conversation is one where it might feel a little more natural. Try asking:

What was most useful from this conversation for you?

This question does two things:

1. It gives you some feedback so you can adapt for next time.
2. It reinforces the learning and actions your team member is taking away.

Suggested experiments

- Be curious about the careers of people close to you. You could ask them some of the questions in this chapter or ask what they wanted to be when they grew up. Their answers will give you an insight into many and varied career paths that can help you guide your team members. It's low risk because friends and family won't have any expectations of you about developing their career as a team member might.

- Try asking 'What was most useful from this meeting for you?' at the end of your next team meeting to gain insight into what's working.

Career conversations

Summary

- You're not responsible for your team member's career; they are.

- Give your team member a choice about whether or not to have a career conversation.

- Set aside specific times for career conversations outside of usual catch-ups – and make it twice a year as a minimum.

- To understand their motivations and values, ask your team member to describe their career to date.

- To know what's important to them, ask your team member to describe what they want their career to look like in the future. Get them to write this down so they can refer back to it when making career decisions.

- Ask questions about their career now to help them plan their next steps.

- To get feedback and reinforce their learning and action, ask 'What was most useful from this conversation for you?'

12 Performance appraisals

No one feels great when they're being judged and we all know that's what a performance appraisal is: a judgement about your team member's performance that influences their future pay and prospects. Add to the mix that money is a touchy subject for us all and that most managers don't want to upset their team members and it's no wonder research by Gallup suggests that performance appraisals can do more harm than good (Sutton & Wigert 2019).

In this chapter, I'll show you how to approach performance appraisals in a coach-like way so that it's developmental for your team, gives you an insight into how to manage them and leads to greater retention.

Co-create a performance appraisal container

In Chapter 7, I showed you how to use the 'ask first, tell last' principle to create a container to delegate using the 'ask, add' pattern to encourage your team member to take responsibility. The same pattern works to create a performance appraisal container because it shows your team member that it's being done *with* them and not *to* them. This is how it works:

Ask: *What would work best for you to have this performance appraisal conversation?*
Add: *Your ideas on how the process could work.*
Ask: *What would you like to get out of this discussion?*
Add: *What you'd like to get from the discussion.*
Ask: *Where would you like to start?*

And this is what it might look like in real life:

You: *What would work best for you to have this performance appraisal conversation?*
Team member: *I'd like to go through it one goal at a time, bringing in the relevant feedback as we go.*
You: *Sounds good to me. I'd like you to do a self-appraisal first before we look at feedback and then I'll add my thoughts. Is that OK?*
Team member: *Yes.*
You: *What would you like to get out of this discussion?*
Team member: *I'd like to know my chances of being promoted next year.*
You: *OK, I can't promise promotion because there*

are so many factors that feed into that, not just your performance. But I can tell you where you're already demonstrating that you're operating at a higher level and where you need to do some work.
Team member: *OK, that makes sense.*
You: *All right. Where would you like to start?*

Like delegating, a performance appraisal conversation is one where you'll have thoughts, opinions and advice that are valuable to share. You'll dance back and forth between coaching and mentoring. When there's a developmental opportunity for your team member, move over to the coaching side. When you have information they need to know, move to the mentoring side.

Give difficult feedback

In Chapter 9 I showed you how to use the principle of letting your team member lead the conversation to frame and ask for permission to share difficult feedback. Framing the feedback prepares your team member for what they're about to hear and lets them know you're on their side. Asking for permission gives them the choice to hear it and also focuses their mind on what you're saying. This is an example frame you can adapt:

I have some feedback on this that might be hard to hear. I'd like to share it with you and then hear your perspective. Are you ready to hear it now?

Be sure to wait for your team member to say 'yes' before you go on, otherwise you'll break the psychological safety gained by asking for permission. By telling them you want to hear their perspective, you're signalling that you know there's more than one side to a story and that increases psychological safety.

Developmental questions for performance appraisals

Performance appraisals are part of the ongoing career conversations you have with your team member (see Chapter 11). Using developmental questions such as these helps your team member to assess the past year and take what they've learned into the next.

> *What are you most proud of this year?*
> *Which strengths did you use the most this year?*
> *What were your biggest challenges this year and how did you overcome them?*
> *What are you most disappointed about?*
> *What do you wish people knew about your performance?*
> *Describe the ways in which you're different today compared to this time last year.*
> *What have you learned about yourself?*

Most of the time you'll find your team member is much harder on themselves than they need to be, so use this opportunity to emphasise their strengths and use your mentoring skills to tell them how much progress they've made.

What to do if your team member gets upset

In Chapter 10, I showed you how you can use a coach-like approach to give your team member space to express what they're feeling. Remember:

- Take a breath and pause; their reaction isn't your fault.
- Listen, don't fix; they don't need to be rescued.
- Let them lead what happens next – they might need a time-out or they might be OK to keep going.

Suggested experiments

- Talk to your team members before performance appraisal time and do some contracting (see Chapter 1) to agree your expectations of one another and how to handle difficult feedback.
- Send developmental questions to your team before their appraisal so they can prepare.

Summary

- Co-create a container for the performance appraisal conversation using the 'ask, add' pattern so that your team member feels you're doing the appraisal together.

- Use framing and asking for permission to prepare your team member for difficult feedback before sharing it.

- Ask developmental questions that will help your team member reflect on what they've learned from the past year to bring it into the next.

- When your team member is being too hard on themselves, reinforce all the positives from the year.

- If your team member gets upset, be with them as they express themselves and ask them how they want to continue.

13 Turning thinking into action

When your team member finds their own solutions, they're often highly motivated to finish the conversation and get on with it. At other times, if there are a lot of actions or there's a lot going on, it can be helpful to ask your team member to tell you their plan. That way you can help them be specific about how they're going to turn their thinking into action.

The time to offer your support is after you've done this. Initially, participants on coaching workshops think it's mean to hold back your offer of help until the end – until they give it a go themselves. By waiting, you stop offering help that your team member doesn't need.

What's your next step?

One of the benefits of being a coach-like manager is that it creates commitment and responsibility in your team members because they take ownership of what happens next. It's the same when you tell a friend you're going for a run – then you have to go. The trick here is to get your team member to be specific about the day, time and place they're going to take action, so there's no doubt:

> *What's your next step?*
> *What day and time are you going to do that?*
> *Where are you going to do that?*

The more specific your team member is – for example, 10 am on Thursday while they're working from home – the more likely they'll take action. With vague times such as 'by the end of the week', it's easier for them to rationalise putting it off and then they might not get round to it. If you want to increase their chances of success, you could also ask:

> *What might get in the way?*
> *How might we remove that obstacle?*

This is a double whammy because, by getting your team member to anticipate what could get in the way, you help them prepare for it. You also get a chance to pick up on potential problems early on and gain insight into how to manage them more effectively to help them succeed.

What help do you need from me?

Let your team member ask for the help they need from you so that they continue to lead the conversation. It also helps you reduce your workload because you're not taking on actions your team member doesn't need.

There's no obligation to give them all the help they ask for. You might suggest alternatives or refer them to others. You don't even need to agree to any support in the moment; you could say you need to consider what you're best placed to do and ask to come back to them.

The important thing to remember when you're being coach-like is that it's not your responsibility to save your team member. They're all resourceful adults. Let them ask for the help they need instead of burdening them with the help you decide they need.

Tell your team member what you appreciate them for

People think best in the presence of genuine appreciation (Kline 2011). It makes sense, right? You're unlikely to do your best thinking or feel safe enough to share if you get criticised all the time. So finish the conversation by telling your team member what you appreciate about them.

Appreciation works best when it's short, specific and you mean it. For example, 'I want to appreciate you for your persistence.' It's as simple and as difficult as that – simple because you only need to name one quality you appreciate in your team member; and difficult because in organisations we're not used to appreciating each other or think we're doing it all the time when in fact we're not.

Telling someone they've done a 'good job' is lovely praise but it's not that specific. It doesn't tell someone what's 'good' about what they're doing so they know to keep doing it.

You might find that some people find it hard to accept appreciation because they have low confidence and self-esteem. According to psychologist Guy Winch (2016), learning to accept compliments helps to increase self-esteem, so if your team member dismisses it, repeat the appreciation to give your team member another chance to hear it. Even if they don't believe it initially, in time the compulsion to dismiss appreciation will fade, which is an indication that their self-esteem is improving.

Suggested experiments

- Take a moment now and make a list of each of your team members. Write down a quality you appreciate in each of them and tell them in your next one-to-one catch-up.

- Choose one technique from Part 2 you'd like to try and write down who you'll use it with and when.

Summary

- Ask your team member what they're going to do next and help them be specific about when and where.

- Ask your team member what help they need from you so that they have a choice over what support you give.

- Tell your team member what quality you appreciate in them to help build their confidence and self-esteem.

14. A way to practise with others

A great way to develop your coaching confidence is to practise with others – and you'll also get the added benefit of coaching for your own career development. This chapter suggests a structure to come together as pairs or trios to learn from each other in a space where it's OK to experiment and stumble.

Contracting

In Chapter 1, I talked about contracting as a way to create psychological safety. This is especially important when practising coaching because everyone will feel vulnerable. The first time you come together, allow extra time so that you can go through each of the items below. After that, make sure to check back in on the contract in each practice session in case something needs to be changed or added.

- Confidentiality – everyone should state what that means for them and what's OK and not OK to share outside the practice session.

- Logistics – how often you'll meet, where, for how long and how the time will be divided up.

- Cancellations and reschedules – how will you manage these?

- Feedback – agree your intentions for giving and receiving feedback. For example, it's intended to help each other develop, not to cut each other down. The guide below has some suggested questions you can use that are developmental and positive.

- What you need the group to know so you can be present – for example, you might be waiting for a call, there might be loud work happening near you, you might be feeling distracted by work that needs to be done.

Write the contract down and share it with everyone to look at before future practice sessions as a reminder.

Practice roles

- The coach – the person doing the asking.

- The thinker – the person with something to think about.

- The observer – the person who takes notes and manages time and feedback. (Pairs won't have an observer.)

Each person will get a chance to be in each role, so it's important that everyone brings a topic to be coached on that's real for them. It could be something that's been on your mind for a while, a challenge you're facing or something you're stuck on.

The coach

It can feel daunting to be the coach when you know you're being observed and will get feedback. Remember that's why you're doing this and you're with people who feel the same as you. You can't get it wrong. The fact that you're even trying means that the conversation will be different and more helpful than what you might have done before.

The thinker

You get to relax a little and benefit from some coaching to help you with an issue or something you're stuck with. Bring something that's real for you now, not a problem you had in the past that's now resolved or something you've made up. A big part of coaching is being present with the thinker and trusting your intuition, which you can't do with a fake topic.

The observer

If you can be in a trio, I highly recommend it because you learn as much from observing coaching as you do being the coach or thinker. Watch the coaching demonstration at coachingtwostep.com/demo to experience what I mean.

The observer's role is to take notes on what they notice during the practice, manage the time and lead the feedback. Prompts about what to take notes on are in the guide that follows. To manage the feedback, first ask the coach their thoughts, then the thinker and, finally, add your observations. The coach is likely to be hard on themselves so make sure they're being balanced. Reflective questions you can use to do this are in the guide below.

Appreciation

Finish each practice session by appreciating each other for a quality you noticed in them during the session. Chapter 13 has more detail on appreciation and its impact.

I appreciate you for your [insert quality you appreciate].

Timing

Here are some suggestions about how to divide the time as a pair or a trio. You can scale the times up or down depending on the amount of time you have.

If you're a pair practising for 60 minutes:

A way to practise with others

Minutes	Activity
9	Greetings; check in on contract and decide who coaches first.
15	Coaching practice for first coach.
8	First thinker leads the feedback by asking the coach: *What went well?* *What would have made it even better?* Thinker then adds their thoughts on: *Who did the most talking – coach or thinker?* *What questions did the coach ask that inspired new thoughts?* *What else might it be useful for the coach to reflect on?*
15	Coaching practice for second coach.
8	Second thinker leads the feedback using the same structure as above.
5	Share an appreciation with each other and say your goodbyes.

If you're a trio practising for 80 minutes:

Minutes	Activity
9	Greetings; check in on contract and decide on roles for the first round.
15	Coaching practice for first coach.
7	First observer leads the feedback by asking the thinker and then the coach: *What went well?* *What would have made it even better?* The observer then adds their thoughts on: *Who did the most talking – coach or thinker?* *What questions did the coach ask that inspired new thoughts?* *What else might it be useful for the coach to reflect on?*
15	Coaching practice for second coach.
7	Second observer leads the feedback as above.
15	Coaching practice for third coach.
7	Third observer leads the feedback as above.
5	Share an appreciation with each other and say your goodbyes.

Conclusion

I want to take a moment to appreciate you for making an effort to learn something new to develop your team. Now take that learning and turn it into action by choosing something that resonated strongly with you and giving it a go. Perhaps you'll try the Coaching Two-Step or pick one of the principles to guide you in a conversation this week. Remember they are:

- Listen, don't fix.
- Ask first, tell last.
- Your team member leads the conversation.

Maybe you'll focus on the quality of your attention or, like Sami in the introduction, you'll see an opportunity to be coach-like and give it a go. Whatever you choose, remember you can't get it wrong.

To keep learning more sign up to my weekly blog of practical coaching ideas you can use every day at thinkwithjude.com/signmeup and follow me on linkedin.com/in/judesclater. If after reading this and trying coaching for yourself you decide you want to train to be a coach, go to thinkwithjude.com/recommendations for suggestions of reputable training organisations.

The lasting impact of being a coach-like manager

The effects of coaching are longer lasting than you might think. As I was writing this book, a colleague I'd worked with more than four years ago sent me this message:

'I have to tell you, sometimes, when I doubt myself, your voice and the questions you'd ask me come into my head. It unlocks my thoughts and tells me to look at the positives.'

That's the kind of long-lasting change in behaviour that happens when you choose to take a coach-like approach rather than defaulting to telling people what to do.

Bring the Coaching Two-Step into your organisation

The jump from technical expert to managing a team of technical experts can feel enormous for new managers. You want to empower your team but fear losing control if you delegate.

The Coaching Two-Step helps you overcome this by showing you how to use everyday conversations to get your team doing their best work.

From a keynote to a webinar or workshop, Think with Jude can tailor a programme that builds managers' confidence to give coaching a go.

To find out more email jude@thinkwithjude.com and let's find time to chat.

Question bank

The questions below are from the previous chapters, collected together with other coach-like wording to give you examples for quick reference.

Chapter 1: How to become a coach-like manager

Ask what they need:

Do you want me to just listen, offer advice, coach you or something else?

To switch from coaching to mentoring:

I know something here that might help – can I share it with you?

I've had some experience of working with them – would it be useful if I told you about it?

This has happened to me too. Do you want to hear what I did?

(Wait to hear 'yes' before continuing.)

To switch from mentoring to coaching:

What are your thoughts?
What do you think?
How might this help with your issue?

Contracting:
Ask: *How often do you want to catch up and for how long?*
Add: *Your thoughts.*
Ask: *How do you want us to structure our catch-ups?*
Add: *Your thoughts.*
Ask: *What would be useful for me to know about how you like to work?*
Add: *What would be useful for your team member to know about how you like to work.*
Ask: *What do you expect from me?*
Add: *What you expect of your team member.*
Ask: *What should we do if we feel like things aren't working between us?*
Add: *Your thoughts.*

Chapter 2: The Coaching Two-Step

Other ways to ask 'Tell me more':
What else?
Say more.
What more do you want to say?
What do you feel about that?
What do you think about that?
What's most important for you?
How would you summarise that?

To offer support:
What support would you like from me?

Chapter 3: Coach-like questions

Outcome focused:

What's your ideal outcome?
What do you want to happen here?
What's the best outcome for you?
What would you be seeing happen if you got this outcome?
What would you be feeling if you got this outcome?
What would you be hearing if you got this outcome?

Examples of using 'might':

How might we see this situation differently?
Who might be able to help us with this?
Where else might we be able to get what we need?

Chapter 4: Coaching in five minutes or less

Outcome focused:

What's the question we need to answer?
What do you want to get from this conversation?
Where do you want to be by the end of this conversation?

To interrupt:

I'm sorry to interrupt; I notice we have two minutes left. What would be most useful for us to do in this time?

Chapter 5: Problem solving

Outcome-focused:

In an ideal world, what would happen?
If we could wave a magic wand, what would be different tomorrow?
If it was an ideal day, what would it look like?
What do you want to achieve?
What do you really want?

To uncover assumptions:

What might you be assuming that's getting in the way of [insert wording of ideal outcome]? What else?
Which assumption is most getting in your way? Tell me more.
I'd really like to [fill in the blank], but [fill in the blank].

To get unstuck:

What advice would you give to a friend with a similar problem?
What would you do if I wasn't here?
What might you do if there were no limits?
If you knew you couldn't fail, what might you do?

Chapter 6: Goal setting

To make a goal meaningful:

What's the dream?
What would achieving this goal enable you to do?
What about the goal is so important for you?

What would it mean to you [to your family, friends, team, organisation] to achieve this?
What would be different if you achieved this?
What would you have that you don't have now?
How will it feel to achieve your goal?
Imagine you've achieved your goal. What would you be seeing and hearing?
If you were to frame that goal in the positive what would that be?
What would it sound like if your goal was ten words or fewer?

To make a goal measurable:
How will we know when you've achieved your goal?
On a scale of 1 to 10, 1 being low and 10 being high, how close to [insert memorable goal wording] are you right now?
Where do you want to be this time next year?

To make a goal memorable:
What word or phrase best summarises the essence of your goal?
What would make this memorable for you?
What does your goal remind you of?
If your goal were a [insert their interest here]. What would it be?

To offer support:
How can I best support you?
Where else can you get support?
How do you want to catch up about these goals?

Chapter 7: Delegating

Co-create a delegating container:
Ask: *How would you like me to brief you?*
Add: *Your thoughts.*
Ask: *What else do you think you'll need?*
Add: *Your thoughts, if any.*

To check understanding:
What questions do you have?
What are your thoughts on how you'll approach this?
What concerns do you have?
What challenges do you see already?
What else do you need to know from me?
What else are you working on and how might that impact this project/task?
Which of your strengths are you going to draw on for this?
What do you want to learn from this?
What skills or knowledge do you think you need to do this that you don't have yet?

Chapter 8: Catching up

For self-evaluation:

The last time we spoke about this you said you were a 4 on a scale of 1 to 10. Where are you now? Then: *What did you do that got you there?* Then: *What would make it a [one number higher]?*

What are you most happy about?

What's working well and why?

What are you learning about yourself?

What challenges have you overcome and how?

What strengths are you noticing? Where else could you be using these?

If you could do it again, what would you do differently?

How are you going to celebrate your success?

To identify challenges and blockers:

What's been the hardest bit?

What challenges are you facing?

What are you stuck on?

To get feedback:

Where would you like me to be more or less involved?

What do you see me getting involved in that I don't need to?

Permission to switch from coaching to mentoring:

Can I make a suggestion?

Can I share something I'm noticing?

I know something that might help here. Can I share it?

Would it be helpful if I told you how I've done this in the past?
Can I tell you about what's not working for me?
Can I share what I'd like to see you doing more of?
(Wait to hear 'yes' before continuing.)

To switch from mentoring to coaching:
How might that be useful for you?
What has changed for you now you've heard that?
What ideas have come to mind now?

Before you complete the catch-up:
What else do you want to talk about?

Chapter 9: Feedback

To frame feedback and ask for permission:
Example: *I want to tell you about something that's affecting your chances of promotion because if it were me I'd want to know so I could do something about it. Before I do, I want you to know that I'm here to support you in any way I can. Do you want to hear it?*

Chapter 10: Strong emotions

To start the conversation:
What's on your mind?
What's up?
What's going on?

Question bank

To acknowledge and explore feelings:
That sounds really hard; thanks for telling me.
What are these feelings telling you?

To offer support:
What help would be most useful from me right now?
Where else are you getting support?
Who else can you get support from?

Chapter 11: Career conversations

To learn from career history:
What are you most proud of in your career?
If you could go back, what would you change?
How did you make the decision to move roles or organisations?
What did changing roles or organisations tell you about what you like or dislike about work?
What has your career to date taught you?

To be clear on future career:
Describe your dream career.
What would you like your career to look like in the future?
What do you want more of in your career?
What do you want less of in your career?

Career planning:
What's going well in your career?
Where would you like to focus your attention?

What skills do you want to develop?
What opportunities do you need?
Who do you need to build stronger relationships with?

To get feedback:
What was most useful from this conversation for you?

Chapter 12: Performance appraisals

Co-create a performance appraisal container:
Ask: *What would work best for you to have this performance appraisal conversation?*
Add: *Your ideas on how the process could work.*
Ask: *What would you like to get out of this discussion?*
Add: *What you'd like to get from the discussion.*
Ask: *Where would you like to start?*

To frame feedback and ask for permission:
I have some feedback on this that might be hard to hear. I'd like to share it with you and then hear your perspective. Are you ready to hear it now?

Developmental questions:
What are you most proud of this year?
Which strengths did you use the most this year?
What were your biggest challenges this year and how did you overcome them?
What are you most disappointed about?
What do you wish people knew about your performance?

Describe the ways in which you're different today compared to this time last year?
What have you learned about yourself?

Chapter 13: Turning thinking into action

To decide next steps:
What's your next step?
What day and time are you going to do that?
Where are you going to do that?
What might get in the way?
How might we remove that obstacle?

To offer support:
What help do you need from me?

To show appreciation:
I appreciate you for your [quality you appreciate in that person].

Resources

Introduction

Whitmore, J (2017) *Coaching for Performance: The principles and practice of coaching and leadership.* 5th ed. Nicholas Brealey, p 39.

Chapter 1: How to become a coach-like manager

Adams, M (2022) *Change Your Questions, Change Your Life: 10 powerful tools for life and work.* 4th ed. Berett-Koehler Publishers, p 64.

Downey, M (2015) *Effective Modern Coaching: The principles and art of successful business coaching.* LID Publishing. p 114.

Edmondson, A (2014) 'Building a psychologically safe workplace'. TEDxHGSE 5 May 2014. URL: youtube.com/watch?v=LhoLuui9gX8

Milner, J & Milner, T (2018) 'Most managers don't know how to coach people. But they can learn'. *Harvard Business Review* 16 August 2018. URL: https://hbr.org/2018/08/most-managers-don't-know-how-to-coach-people-but-they-can-learn

Pedrick, C (2021) *Simplifying Coaching: How to have*

more transformational conversations by doing less. Open University Press, McGraw Hill, p 124.

Chapter 2: The Coaching Two-Step

Black, O & Bailey, S (2009) *The Mind Gym: Relationships.* Sphere, p 78.

Jha, A (2021) *Peak Mind: Find your focus, own your attention, invest 12 minutes a day.* Hachette UK, p 34.

Mannix, K (2021) *Listen: How to find the words for tender conversations.* HarperCollins UK, pp 29, 117.

Norman, C (2022) *The Transformational Coach: Free your thinking and break through to coaching mastery.* The Right Book Company, pp 241–242.

Varol, O (n.d.) '3 counterintuitive ways to excel in conversation'. URL: ozanvarol.com/3-counterintuitive-ways-to-excel-in-conversation

Chapter 4: Coaching in five minutes or less

Kline, N (2011) *Time to Think: Listening to ignite the human mind.* Octopus, p 55.

Chapter 6: Goal setting

Locke, E & Latham, G (2002) 'Building a practically useful theory of goal setting and task motivation. A 35-year odyssey'. *American Psychologist* 57. URL: researchgate.net/publication/11152729_

Building_a_practically_useful_theory_of_goal_setting_and_task_motivation._A_35-year_odyssey._American_Psychologist_57

Chapter 7: Delegating

Varol, O (n.d.) 'Yes, there are stupid questions'. URL: ozanvarol.com/yes-there-are-stupid-questions

Chapter 9: Feedback

Bergland, C (2019) 'Longer exhalations are an easy way to hack your vagus nerve: Respiratory vagus nerve stimulation (rVNS) counteracts fight-or-flight stress'. *Psychology Today* 9 March 2019. URL: psychologytoday.com/us/blog/the-athletes-way/201905/longer-exhalations-are-easy-way-hack-your-vagus-nerve

Brown, B (2018) 'Clear is kind. Unclear is unkind'. URL: brenebrown.com/articles/2018/10/15/clear-is-kind-unclear-is-unkind

Peters, S (2013) *The Chimp Paradox: The mind management program to help you achieve success, confidence, and happiness.* TarcherPerigee, pp 27–30.

Chapter 10: Strong emotions

Bungay Stanier, M (2016) *The Coaching Habit: Say less, ask more & change the way you lead forever.* Box of Crayons Press, pp 36–48.

Burn, A (2020) 'The benefits of taking coaching conversations outdoors – what the research says'. URL: alexburnconsulting.com/the-benefits-of-taking-coaching-conversations-outdoors-what-the-research-says

David, S (2018) 'The gift and power of emotional courage'. TED 20 February 2018. URL: youtube.com/watch?v=NDQ1Mi5I4rg

Fosslien, L & West Duffy, M (2019) *No Hard Feelings: The secret power of embracing emotions at work.* Portfolio, pp 80–92.

Weir, K (2021) 'Nurtured by nature'. *American Psychological Association* 1 April. URL: apa.org/monitor/2020/04/nurtured-nature

Chapter 11: Career conversations

LHH (2022) 'Global Workforce of the Future 2022: Unravelling the talent conundrum'. URL: info.lhh.com/GBL/LD-global-workforce-of-the-future-2022

Chapter 12: Performance appraisals

Sutton, R & Wigert, B (2019) 'More harm than good: The truth about performance reviews'. Gallup. URL: gallup.com/workplace/249332/harm-good-truth-performance-reviews.aspx

Chapter 13: Turning thinking into action

Winch, G (2016) '5 ways to build lasting self-esteem'. Ideas.Ted.com, 23 August. URL: ideas.ted.com/5-ways-to-build-lasting-self-esteem

Acknowledgements

I want to appreciate all the people who helped me get this book into your hands. They gave me encouragement, feedback, places to test my ideas and most of all they believed in me.

To Alice Williams, Andrew Chapman, Beverley Glick, Boaz Safir, Christina Wedgewood, Clare Hill, Clare Norman, Collette Harvey, Dave Taylor, Dina Zavali, Esther Stanhope, Fernanda De Silva, Geoff Hardy, Guy Johnson, Helen Buckwell, Helen Waite, Holly Jones, Honey Clarke, Kate Anslow, Kim Arnold, Liz Walker, Lucy Dawson-McGrath, Mary Hobbins, Paul East, Rob Dighton, Michelle Sclater, Nick Redeyoff, Petrana Zemanova, Sonia Keneally, Sue Richardson, Tee Twyford, Verity Craft, Vicki Kassioula and all my subscribers and followers... Thank you.

Extra thanks go to my husband Rob Sclater, who makes everything beautiful.

About the author

Coach and writer Jude Sclater works with leading organisations – including global consulting firms, law firms, investment managers, consumer foods and more – to help them develop great managers that people want to work for. An ex IT auditor and project manager, she holds an MSc in Organisational Behaviour from Birkbeck University and is an accredited practitioner coach through the European Mentoring and Coaching Council.

When she's not coaching, she's working hard on transforming her garden, creating home-made pizzas with her husband and learning the art of wine tasting. You can subscribe to her weekly blog, which shows you how to think like a coach so that you too can be a great manager, at thinkwithjude.com/signmeup.